Arms, Money, and Politics

Arms, Money, and Politics

by
JULIUS DUSCHA

IVES WASHBURN, INC.

New York

ARMS, MONEY, AND POLITICS

LIBRARY OF CONGRESS CATALOG CARD NUMBER: 65-20066

MANUFACTURED IN THE UNITED STATES OF AMERICA

VAN REES PRESS • NEW YORK

For

Priscilla,

Fred, Steve, Sue, and Sally

Contents

Contents

Foreword

THE MAJOR FORCE working for large defense budgets in the United States today is not the military, powerful as it has become during the last twenty-five years. Nor is it the eighteen thousand corporations holding defense contracts, the thousands of subcontractors, or the thousands of communities that depend on defense plants and military bases for their prosperity. Rather, the major force for armament is the American people's massive distrust of the Soviet Union. It is an overwhelmingly justifiable fear based on the Soviet record of aggression and broken agreements.

But the 7 million Americans who depend directly on defense spending also know that large military programs mean continued employment for them. For every person directly involved in the defense efforts, there are from one to three others who have jobs providing goods and services for officers and enlisted men, for defense plant employees and executives. Thus the livelihood of at least 14 million American families is directly or indirectly tied to a high level of military expenditure.

This book is an effort to consider the economic and political problems that have become an integral part of the defense program. It does not start from the premise that military spending remains at levels of nearly $50 billion a year because of a conspiracy among the generals, admirals, and businessmen who profit in prestige as well as money from a large defense program. Rather, it is an attempt to take a realistic look at the politics and economics of defense spending and to propose solutions for at least some of the problems raised by defense spending.

In both the Soviet Union and the United States defense spending appears to be leveling off. Therefore the problems involved in the transition of the American economy from one dependent on large peacetime expenditures to one less dependent on defense spending will have to be faced by all Americans. If this book contributes in some way to recognition of these political and economic problems and discussion of ways to solve them, the author's purpose will have been served.

This book grew out of a suggestion to the author by John Fischer, the editor of *Harper's Magazine,* for a series of articles on what former President Eisenhower called "the military-industrial complex." The articles appeared in *Harper's* in the spring of 1964. The material used in these articles has been greatly expanded and incorporated into this book.

JULIUS DUSCHA

CHEVY CHASE, MARYLAND
FEBRUARY 1965

Arms, Money, and Politics

CHAPTER 1

Congress and Defense Spending

SENATOR GAYLORD NELSON of Wisconsin was on his feet seeking recognition by the presiding officer. Nelson had no trouble gaining the Senate floor even though he was only a freshman senator. It was February 1964 and the Senate had just taken final action on a bill reducing federal income taxes by $11 billion and was about to give quick consideration to two other seemingly unrelated measures before moving on to what would be a lengthy debate on civil rights legislation. The tax bill had been under discussion on Capitol Hill for more than a year, and it was with a sense of relief that the senators momentarily turned their attention to what they considered less important matters.

"The United States Senate," Nelson began, "has just approved the final conference report on the largest tax reduction in American history.... The Senate and the House—and the American public—have spent much of the past year debating this step. Every aspect of it has been thoroughly scrutinized in free and open debate inside and outside the Congress.

"During this long debate one point has been made over and over: If we are to make this massive reduction in federal tax

I

revenues, we must at the same time take a long and careful look at federal spending, so that we know and the American public knows that we are acting as responsible officials.

"I find it ironic, therefore, that at this moment, hard on the heels of this massive tax-cut plan, we are asked to approve a $17 billion military authorization bill, the biggest authorization bill in American history, with almost no consideration and no real debate by the United States Senate. . . .

"Why are we expected," Nelson asked, "to pass this bill in two or three hours—before the committee hearings on the bill have even been printed; before any senator not on the Senate Armed Services Committee has had an opportunity to study the testimony on the bill; within twenty-four hours after we had an opportunity at all to know even what the Senate Armed Services Committee recommended; before any of us have had an opportunity to compare the committee's recommendations with the proposals of the administration and witnesses before the committee? . . .

"We do not follow this procedure on foreign aid. We do not simply take the word of the President, or the Agency for International Development, or even the Senate Foreign Relations Committee and its distinguished chairman. We spend weeks debating the foreign aid bill, and we cut it by a billion dollars or more. . . .

"I am questioning," Nelson said, "what is apparently an established tradition, perhaps a national attitude, which holds that a bill to spend billions of dollars for the machinery of war must be rushed through the House and the Senate in a matter of hours, while a treaty to advance the cause of peace, or a program to help the underdeveloped nations of the world, or a bill to guarantee the rights of all our citizens, or a bill to advance the interests of the poor must be scrutinized and debated and amended and thrashed over for weeks and perhaps months."

Nelson noted that most of the $17 billion in expenditures the Senate was being asked to authorize would go for the purchase of 53 ships, 2,700 airplanes, and 35,000 missiles. "Are we increasing American security?" Nelson asked. "Or are we simply adding to our overkill possibilities?" The questions went unanswered, because by the time Nelson had asked them, the Senate chamber was all but empty. Nelson was discovering what another freshman senator had found out in the fall of 1963: Congress simply does not want to probe into the details of defense spending, which amounts to almost $50 billion a year and accounts for nearly 10 percent of all the goods and services produced in the United States in a single year.

One lazy afternoon in September 1963, Senator George McGovern of South Dakota (who like Nelson came to the Senate in 1963) stood at his back-row desk in an almost empty Senate chamber and suggested that defense spending could be reduced without endangering the national security.

McGovern is a mild-mannered man who was director of the Food-for-Peace program under President Kennedy before entering the Senate. A former political science professor with a distinguished World War II record as a bomber pilot, McGovern had long been concerned about defense spending. As a member of the House of Representatives for two terms during the late 1950's, he had considered making a determined effort to challenge items in the defense budget, but as an exceedingly junior member of Congress, he had held back in deference to the ruling elders of the House who wanted as little debate as possible over defense budgets.

McGovern first questioned defense spending in August 1963 in a speech entitled "New Perspectives on American Security." He suggested that the United States already had more nuclear warheads than it could conceivably use; that it is less dangerous to try to bring the arms race under control than it is to proliferate nuclear weapons; that present levels of military spending are distorting the United States economy and wasting human resources; and that by diverting some of the money being spent on military programs to other investments, the quality of people's lives could be vastly improved. His speech brought much favorable comment from newspapers and interested citizens across the country, but it hardly created a ripple on Capitol Hill.

With his August speech serving as a prologue, McGovern stood on the Senate floor the following September when the defense appropriations bill was under consideration and said:

"We are considering in this one bill today half the entire budget of the United States government. It represents 10 percent of the gross national product of the American people. It is five and a half times as large as the entire budget of the United States government in 1940. It is equal to the combined total of all the federal budgets during the New Deal period from 1933 until 1940."

McGovern went on to say that he would offer an amendment to the bill that would reduce by 10 percent the money being made available for the procurement of weapons and for the Defense Department's research and development funds.

"Nearly two years ago," McGovern reminded the Senate, "Secretary McNamara expressed the conviction that we had more than enough nuclear weapons to destroy the enemy even after absorbing a first strike. . . .

"Yet the bill now before us calls for additional billions to add new force and refinements to our retaliatory power. A significant portion of the procurement expense in this proposed appropriation is for more missiles. A heavy part of the proposed research and development is aimed at new styles of nuclear devices—medium range mobile missiles, tactical nuclear artillery, and a bewildering array of sophisticated, highly expensive modifications.

"Over half a billion dollars is included in this bill for battlefield tactical nuclear devices. We already have ten thousand nuclear weapons in Europe, which is enough to insure the death of the continent if war should come. Actually, these weapons

4

are a threat to our security rather than a safeguard. Their presence in Europe almost guarantees that any conflict which develops there would escalate into a nuclear exchange between Russia and ourselves. As they proliferate, we increase the risk that one of them may one day set off a conflagration that could destroy Western society. Adding hundreds of millions of dollars to this tactical nuclear weapons force is literally courting disaster—and wasting an enormous volume of tax dollars."

McGovern pointed out that even with the $2.2 billion reduction in spending that he was advocating, the armed services would still have more than $50 billion available to them during the 1964 fiscal year and that the United States would still have seven hundred B-52 and B-58 bombers, hundreds of B-47's, more than one thousand intercontinental ballistic missiles, and thirty-five Polaris submarines carrying 560 missiles.

Concluding that "this is hardly a blueprint for pacifism," McGovern added: "Any single one of these several thousand nuclear delivery systems is capable of unleashing more explosive power than all the explosives of World War II combined, from friend and foe alike. Any single bomb or warhead in the fantastic stockpiles that we have been building for eighteen years would make the Hiroshima bomb look like a child's toy."

Only one senator replied to McGovern's argument, but he was Senator Richard B. Russell of Georgia, the chairman of both the Senate Armed Services Committee and the Senate Defense Appropriations Subcommittee.

Russell is a patrician Georgia bachelor with a haughty, superior manner. He has been in the Senate for thirty years and is the leader of the Southern bloc. Russell's own state of Georgia has so many military installations it has been said that the location of another base in the state would sink it. The power that Russell has amassed in the Senate probably is due more to his influential position as the official senatorial overseer of the defense establishment than to camaraderie or persuasiveness.

For McGovern and his suggestion that defense spending should be reduced, a suggestion that Senator Jennings Randolph of West Virginia supported with a Senate speech, Russell had only words of scorn and sarcasm.

"I am somewhat saddened," Russell said, "by the two able addresses which have been delivered to the Senate this afternoon. It seems to me we have at least found the germ of confidence in unilateral disarmament, which can only bring this country to its destruction."

Russell was one of a handful of senators who led the opposition to the treaty the Senate had just ratified after a month of debate prohibiting the testing of nuclear weapons in the atmosphere. During the debate, supporters of the treaty had repeatedly asserted that its ratification would not mean any reduction in the nation's defense program; and Russell had made certain that the defense appropriations bill would be considered on the day the test-ban treaty was ratified, knowing that it would be virtually impossible that day to make even a token reduction in defense spending.

"I wish," he went on to say in his reply to McGovern and Randolph, "we were able to reduce drastically the enormous expenditures we make each year for the purposes of national defense. I have seen a number of striking illustrations of what could be done with the money we spend on our military establishment in only two or three years. I have seen stories pointing out that we could give every American family a fine house in which to live, adequate space for the family, two-car garages, cars to go into the garages, and a system of education without parallel in all the history of the human family. It would be a good life and makes utopia sound like a dreary spot indeed.

"I cannot accept that picture," Russell declared, "beautiful and alluring as it is, because if we in this country were to make every man a king and every woman a queen, what would it profit us if the Communists overwhelmed us and took over and enslaved us? I assume the Communist conspiracy would prefer

6

to enslave a generation of queens and kings rather than ordinary people."

Russell concluded that, despite the enormous military expenditures since World War II, there is only "a thin margin of superiority between our military establishment and that of the Soviet Union, so far as we are informed."

"If we should take this much of the muscle from our military establishment," Russell declared, "we would still have a fair military establishment. We would have a strong military establishment, but we would be in the position of a man who has three kings and a pair of treys bucking three aces and a pair of deuces. Nobody has ever yet paid off on the second best poker hand."

The Senate did not want to debate McGovern's proposal. Senators Barry M. Goldwater of Arizona and Howard Cannon of Nevada, both generals in the Air Force reserve, spoke up for their service, and the Senate then went on to defeat the McGovern amendment, by a crushing vote of 74 to 2. Only Randolph voted with McGovern. A short while later the defense appropriations bill was passed. It had been a leisurely afternoon of desultory debate. Except for McGovern's speech, there was none of the probing and sharp questioning that marked the Senate's three-week debate on the foreign aid program, later in the fall of 1963, involving less than 4 percent of the total federal budget.

No one, least of all freshman Senator McGovern, was surprised by the defeat of his rather modest proposal. Not since the country's isolationist days in the 1930's has Congress seriously questioned the need for large defense expenditures—in time of peace as well as war.

McGovern is not, however, a man who gives up easily, even in the face of the powerful senatorial odds arrayed against him; and five months later, in February 1964, he again tried to promote some intelligent debate on defense spending. This time

7

McGovern was joined by Nelson of Wisconsin, who led off the floor debate on the bill authorizing the expenditure of $17 billion on new projects in the year beginning July 1, 1964, and in succeeding fiscal years. (Projects authorized in one year often are not undertaken immediately, and frequently the spending of money for the projects continues over several years. In any single year the expenditures of the Defense Department, which have been around $50 billion annually in recent years, come from funds authorized and appropriated over a period of several preceding years.)

The focus of McGovern's and Nelson's efforts was a $52 million item in the $17 billion authorization bill. The $52 million was placed in the legislation by the House Armed Services Committee—and was accepted by the House and by the Senate Armed Services Committee to help the Air Force in its persistent attempts to develop a new bomber. Secretary of Defense Robert S. McNamara had allowed only $5 million for studies of the feasibility of such a bomber.

The authorization had been increased ten times on Capitol Hill because, in Russell's words, "by providing this sum, the committee is underlining its previously expressed concern that we have no new bomber under development," and also because "the committee continues to think that a combination of missiles and bombers should be in inventory, to be used as our strategic deterrent, rather than to place sole reliance on missiles."

Russell acknowledged, however, that "speaking in all candor, and judging by the experience of the past, it is unlikely that the Department will use all or any substantial part of the additional authorization."

It was General Curtis S. LeMay, then the Air Force Chief of Staff, who convinced first the House and then the Senate Armed Services Committee that more money was needed for the development of a bomber, even though LeMay himself had said in his testimony before the House Armed Services Committee that a formal request for such a bomber program had not been made by the Air Force to Secretary McNamara because "he has asked additional questions of how we intend to use these bombers, what the operational concept is going to be, and how many of them are going to be needed." LeMay conceded that "these are very difficult questions to answer at this particular time."

But only four of the twenty-six members of the House Armed Services Committee dissented from the committee's action to give LeMay what he wanted, even though he was not at all sure what he would do with the money.

"Frankly," said the minority of four, "it is not at all clear to us just what the $52 million is to be spent for, and there is nothing in either the committee report or the testimony to answer this question. Presumably the money is to be used to develop and acquire long lead time items in avionics and engines. But we find it hard to see how funds could be wisely or economically spent on supporting equipment for an aircraft whose configuration and mission had not yet been clearly defined.

"We must be especially careful to guard ourselves," the House minority warned, "against the temptation of building new aircraft just for the sake of building, and before we know how a particular system will be used and precisely how it will be integrated with the ballistic missile force on which we are now concentrating so much of our effort and substance."

McGovern repeated the same warnings when he spoke on the Senate floor. He reminded the Senate that a total of $1.5 billion had been spent in recent years on another bomber that would never fly for the Air Force—the plane called first the B-70 and then the RS-70 when the Air Force decided its bomber project might get further if it were pushed as a reconnaissance aircraft.

As the debate continued, however, it soon became clear that the Air Force's $52 million project would stay aloft, aided by such full-blown oratory as that of Senator A. S. (Mike) Monroney of Oklahoma, who told the Senate: "Few people realize the tragic state of obsolescence of the manned bomber in our Air Force. If they could see the aircraft we now rely upon to carry out the massive raids with thermonuclear weapons, in the event it is necessary to use them; if they could see the old B-47, the gallant old plane being phased out most rapidly, as it becomes too expensive to maintain; if they could see the B-52 with its wings drooping on various airfields of the Air Force, and the difficult fixes put on them to make them airworthy and to give them still a tenuous place in our first line of defense; if they could realize that the B-58, our latest bomber, is out of production; if they realized that the B-47 and the B-52 were designed more than twelve years ago and that something massive must have been learned in the state of the art since then; and if they realized the competent use that could be made of aircraft designs to produce planes to carry the weapons of our arsenal to the enemy, I think they would agree it is time, in 1964, to exercise the talents and the best brains of American aircraft designers to produce a weapon capable of being effectively used, whether in all-out nuclear war or in limited war, or in almost any type of war we might have."

What Monroney neglected to say was that Tulsa, Oklahoma, has a huge government-owned aircraft plant that the Douglas Corporation once operated and all Oklahomans would like to see producing planes—and jobs—again. Monroney, a former newspaperman with a pleasing just-folks manner, also neglected to mention that his state has become accustomed to Air Force bases. The Air Force has always rewarded its friends with bases and contracts, and Monroney has been an advocate of air power ever since he came to the House in the late 1930's.

Arguments such as Monroney's prevailed on that winter's day in February 1964. After the talk had ended and the votes had been counted, McGovern's modest amendment was defeated by the decisive vote of 64 to 20. The twenty votes

McGovern's proposal finally got compared favorably with the two that were cast for his budget-cutting amendment of the previous fall, but twenty is still a long way from a Senate majority.

The $52 million question came up again in April. This time the House of Representatives spent the better part of two afternoons discussing the $46.7 billion defense appropriations bill for the 1965 fiscal year before passing it unanimously. So sluggish was the House debate that members used some of the time allotted for discussion of the defense bill to praise Representative Mike Kirwan of Ohio in a series of self-serving speeches. Kirwan, a Democrat from Cleveland, occupies the politically strategic post of chairman of the House Appropriations subcommittee that handles Interior Department projects. He is the keeper of one of the oldest pork barrels on Capitol Hill. It behooves an up-and-coming member of the house to flatter Kirwan, who has cut off projects in the district of a member incurring his wrath.

In July Senator William Proxmire of Wisconsin tried once again to get the $52 million bomber fund cut back to McNamara's original $5 million request. Proxmire was met with arguments such as the one put forward by Senator Leverett Saltonstall of Massachusetts, the ranking Republican member of the Senate Armed Services Committee, who said: "In cases in which we as members of Congress are charged with the responsibility to appropriate money, in an instance where there is a difference of opinion between two experts—one a civilian and one a military leader, the head of the Air Force—I would rather put the money in and then leave it to them to argue whether the money should be spent rather than to take the responsibility of saying that one man is right."

Admissions like Saltonstall's caused Senator Joseph S. Clark of Pennsylvania to comment: "For a number of years I have been gravely concerned about the way in which the Senate, in almost routine fashion, has accepted without question and without significant debate the recommendations of the Department of Defense and the Appropriations Committee."

Clark also had words of encouragement for McGovern, Proxmire, and Nelson and their efforts to generate on the Senate floor some intelligent discussion of defense spending, but the words spoken and the arguments made by this small band of senators had no effect. Their amendments to cut spending by 2 or by 4 percent or to reduce expenditures for new bomber studies by $47 million (from $52 million to the $5 million requested by McNamara) received the support of no more than eleven senators in July 1964.

Like most other Americans, members of Congress believe that the bigger the defense budget, the safer the country. In today's world there is no question that the United States must spend billions upon billions of dollars to keep up its defenses, but record-breaking defense budgets year after year do not necessarily mean a stronger nation. The bigger any government program gets, the greater the dangers that funds will be wasted and that the goals of the program will become entangled in a morass of vested interests, political considerations, and the rivalries that inevitably evolve. There is no better catharsis for huge government expenditures than informed, skeptical, and continued questioning of these expenditures.

In his valedictory address as President in January 1961, General Eisenhower warned against what he called the military-industrial complex in these words: "The conjunction of an immense military establishment and a large arms industry is new in American experience. The total influence is felt in every city, every state house, every office of the federal government. We recognize the imperative need for this development. Yet we must not fail to comprehend its grave implications. Our toil, resources, and livelihood are all involved; so is the very structure of our society.

"In the councils of government," Eisenhower continued, "we

must guard against the acquisition of unwarranted influence, whether sought or unsought, by the military-industrial complex. The potential for the disastrous rise of misplaced power exists and will persist. We must never let the weight of this combination endanger our liberties or democratic processes. We should take nothing for granted. Only an alert and knowledgeable citizenry can compel the proper meshing of the huge industrial and military machinery of defense with our peaceful methods and goals, so that security and liberty may prosper together."

Despite Eisenhower's clear warning, defense spending remains almost immune from searching criticism in Congress. Defense budgets sail through Congress not solely because senators and representatives are convinced of the need for large military expenditures to keep the Western world safe from the Communists. They also mean jobs for nearly 7 million Americans—almost 10 percent of our working population—and profits for the businesses, large and small, that depend on defense contracts and subcontracts. The senators and representatives who let defense appropriations slide through Congress are quite aware that these funds mean money in the pockets of workers and businessmen back home; and if by chance some members of Congress are not aware of these economic facts, businessmen, chambers of commerce, and labor unions quickly remind them of the importance of defense contracts to their districts and states.

The military-industrial complex is not a sinister cabal. Rather, most of its work is done in the open, and with the enthusiastic support of the American people, a frightening number of whom have the same economic stake in large defense expenditures as do the generals and admirals and the presidents and the chairmen of the boards of the big corporations that build the weapons. Such spending has become an accepted part of American life. In a dozen states defense payrolls account for from 10 to 30 percent of all employment in manufacturing plants. Southern California, one of the fastest-growing areas in the nation, depends on defense contracts to prop up a fourth of its economy, and it is the envy of chambers of commerce everywhere else. The Midwest, which lost defense business to the West during the 1950's as the military emphasis shifted from tanks and airplanes to missiles, is yelling "Foul!" and clamoring for contracts. Midwestern governors may disagree on many issues, but they have banded together to try to get more defense business for their states.

On Capitol Hill, defense contracts are viewed as public works projects. Members of Congress campaign on the basis of their ability to get defense work into their states or districts. "We have reached the point," Representative Jamie L. Whitten, a Mississippi Democrat on the House Defense Appropriations subcommittee, has said, "where tenure of office of a congressman or senator . . . is controlled to a great degree by how many defense contracts he may get back in his own area."

Whenever a big factory is shut or business otherwise falls off in a community, the first thought of its industrialists and labor and political leaders is: How can we get a defense contract? In December 1963, the Studebaker Corporation decided to halt the production of automobiles in South Bend, Indiana, and the state's two Democratic Senators, Vance Hartke and Birch Bayh, and the Democratic Congressman who represents South Bend, John Brademas, immediately issued a statement deploring the action but pointing out how the Pentagon had done all it could to save the faltering Studebaker operation.

"We have been highly pleased with Studebaker's phenomenal record of success as a government contractor," the two Senators and the Congressman noted. "The firm has become a major supplier in just two and a half years. Unranked on the Army's list of top fifty producers until 1962, Studebaker made that list in forty-third postion that year and jumped all the way to twelfth on the Army procurement list in fiscal 1963. There was every indication that Studebaker would continue to be one of the Army's top procurement companies.

"Three reasons for this success stand out," the statement continued. "First, Studebaker had an excellent record of production and on-time delivery for the government, a tribute to the skilled labor force and operating management in South Bend. Second, Studebaker seemed to have a complete understanding of defense procurement and, in bidding and agency contract work, was able to do a better job than competitors. Third, Studebaker obviously received sympathetic consideration on the part of the present administration."

Seldom do members of Congress so openly acknowledge favoritism from the Pentagon and the White House in an effort, in this case unsuccessful, to keep a plant open and to maintain a payroll in a state or congressional district.

Waste in defense spending is tolerated by Congress because the expenditures, however misdirected they may be in terms of national security, still create jobs and profits. In a Senate speech in December 1963 defending Secretary McNamara's efforts to reduce waste in defense programs, Senate Democratic Leader Mike Mansfield of Montana pointed out that in the previous ten years defense projects costing $5 billion had been abandoned as useless.

"To be sure," Mansfield acknowledged, "some value, some experience may well have been obtained from each of them. But let there be no mistake about it. Taken together, they are indicative, to say the least, of an immense and conspicuous consumption of the nation's supply of talent and facilities for research and development. For this technological high living, it is the people of the United States who must pick up the check in actual military costs and in the incalculable costs of a distorted usage of scarce scientific and technological resources."

The address by Mansfield, who is a former professor of

history at the University of Montana and one of the most thoughtful members of the Senate, began as a defense of McNamara but ended with words of solemn warning about the workings of the military-industrial complex.

"I should also like to stress," said Mansfield, "that we are not going to get an effective and efficient defense at a tolerable cost unless it is recognized in all frankness:

"First, that the defense establishment, as the largest single purchaser of goods and services in the nation, has come to occupy a substantial position in the civilian economy of the nation; that, in this connection, what the Defense Department does or does not do has come to have great importance not only for defense but for the well-being of business, labor, and whole communities scattered throughout the nation.

"Second, that in the light of this economic position which the defense establishment occupies, it would be a gross naïveté to assume that pressures, increasing pressures, will not be present for the Defense Department to make decisions not solely on considerations of necessary, effective, and efficient defense—and may I say that colloquies on the floor between senators from various of the larger states underscore this point.

"Third, that however understandable these pressures may be—and as senator from Montana I hope that I try to do as much for my state as any other member—the nation will be ill served if there is not within this government those attitudes and those conditions for administration of the affairs of the defense establishment which permit the decisions, in the end, to be made on the basis of necessary, effective, and efficient defense."

Mansfield noted Eisenhower's warning to the nation of the dangers of the military-industrial complex and then concluded: "If there were ever to be an imminent danger to freedom in this nation of the kind alluded to by Mr. Eisenhower, it is likely to be the consequence of the failure of civilian responsibility in the Congress no less than in the executive branch of the government."

Not only have the vast defense expenditures of the post-World War II years diverted scientists and technicians from civilian pursuits to defense work, billions of tax dollars have also been diverted from such vital needs as education, rapid transportation, the renewal of cities, the retraining of workers made obsolete by automation, the rescue of depressed areas, the prevention of juvenile delinquency, the conservation of natural resources, and the development of facilities for recreation. Ever since the Truman Administration during the late 1940's, federal programs to fulfill needs of the civilian economy have been postponed or cut back to provide funds for defense. For the same reason taxes have also been at high levels.

Throughout most of these years the nation's economy has continued to grow and to change. So different is today's economy from that of the late 1930's that no one knows whether the economy needs defense expenditures to remain prosperous or whether it can exist without what has become an unprecedented prop over the last twenty-five years.

"Of all the changes in American life wrought by the cold war," said Senator J. W. Fulbright of Arkansas, the chairman of the Senate Foreign Relations Committee, in an address given at the University of North Carolina in April 1964, "the most important by far, in my opinion, has been the massive diversion of energy and resources from the creative pursuits of civilized society to the conduct of a costly and interminable struggle for world power. We have been compelled, or have felt ourselves compelled, to reverse the traditional order of our national priorities, relegating individual and community life to places on the scale below the enormously expensive military and space activities that constitute our program of national security.

"At least as striking as the inversion of priorities which the cold war has enforced upon American life," Fulbright continued, "is the readiness with which the American people have consented to defer programs for their welfare and happiness in favor of costly military and space programs. Indeed, if the Congress accurately reflects the temper of the country, then the American people are not only willing, they are eager to sacrifice education and urban renewal and public health programs—to say nothing of foreign aid—to the requirements of the armed forces and the space agency. There is indeed a most striking paradox in the fact that military budgets of over $50 billion are adopted by the Congress after only perfunctory debate, while domestic education and welfare programs involving sums which are mere fractions of the military budget are painstakingly examined and then either considerably reduced or rejected outright. . . .

"To a very considerable extent the American people are not now exercising effective control over the armed forces; nor indeed is the Congress, despite its primary constitutional responsibility in this field. Partly because of anxieties about the cold war, partly because of our extraordinary technological bias, which leads us to place extraordinary faith in the ability of 'technicians' to deal with matters that we ourselves find incomprehensible, and partly because of the vested interests in the 'military-industrial complex,' we are permitting the vast military establishment largely to run itself, to determine its own needs, and to tell us what sacrifices are expected of us to sustain the national arsenal of weapons. . . .

"To the extent that the American people and the Congress shrink from questioning the size and cost of our defense establishment, they are permitting military men, with their highly specialized viewpoints, to make political judgments of the greatest importance regarding the priorities of public policy and the allocation of public funds."

By failing to control or carefully audit defense spending, members of Congress and their constituents have stood complacently by while billions of tax dollars have been wasted in the name of containing Communism. The story of this waste is as shocking as it is difficult to understand in a country where waste was once the worst sin of the frontier life that molded so many Americans and their traditions and values.

CHAPTER 2

Why Billions Are Wasted

NESTLED in the mountains of West Virginia is a $64 million monument to the waste that has become an accepted part of the defense program. The West Virginia fiasco can hardly be seen, and perhaps it is just as well. For their $64 million, American taxpayers did not even get a completed building. All there is to show for the money is a 17,000 cubic yard concrete foundation and a huge, 550-ton bearing on which the Navy's Big Dish was going to turn so that it could scan the heavens from the splendid isolation of Sugar Grove, West Virginia. The story began in 1948 when scientists at the Naval Research Laboratory developed the concept of a large radio telescope that could be carefully steered so it would pick up radio signals from outer space. Work continued on this idea until by 1956 a proposal had been developed for the use of a reflector 600 feet in diameter (quickly named the Big Dish) that could be turned a full 360 degrees and tilted to any angle.

It was surely a spectacular concept. The Big Dish would maintain its position, or change it if desired, automatically. It would have tolerances of a fraction of an inch. Wind, ice, solar and cloud shadow distortion, and other environmental conditions would not disturb the telescope's operations. The reflector could rise to a maximum height of 675 feet and its surface would cover seven acres. Big Dish would weigh thousands of tons and would be the largest movable land-based structure ever built.

With Big Dish the United States would be able to detect galaxies billions of light years from the earth and study them with many times the accuracy of the finest optical telescopes. The Navy has never said so publicly, but by 1956 the plan was to make Big Dish primarily a device that would use the moon as a relay point for monitoring radio transmissions from the Soviet Union.

And all this, said the Navy in 1956, could be done at a cost of only $20 million. Impressed, Congress readily authorized the project and granted the Navy $1.3 million for initial architectural and engineering work. In less than a year, however, the estimated cost of the project more than doubled, and in February 1957 the Navy asked Congress to authorize a total of $52 million in expenditures to build Big Dish. Soon, though, even the $52 million estimate was abandoned as unrealistic, and a $79 million price tag was placed on the project. The Navy explained that Big Dish was more expensive because its concept had been abruptly changed from a limited-use research instrument to a project with highly secret military potentialities. This was a guarded reference to plans for using Big Dish to pick up Soviet radio transmissions.

However secret or essential Big Dish may have been, the Navy could not contain its costs. Soon the Navy acknowledged that the project probably would need $200 million and that the price might even go to $300 million. When a $20 million project becomes a $200 million operation within a few years, it is too much even for Congress to take, and in 1961 the Senate and the House agreed that a $135 million ceiling should be placed on Big Dish. This congressional crackdown prompted the Navy to shut down its construction operations in West Virginia and to concentrate on the completion of the designs for its Sugar Grove project.

By July 1962, however, Secretary McNamara had had enough of Big Dish and ordered cancellation of the project. At that time the Navy had obligated more than $96 million for it and had actually spent nearly $43 million. Two years later the project had not yet been officially terminated (even closing down a project takes time and money), and the General Accounting Office (GAO) estimated in its postmortem on Big Dish that the project would eventually cost taxpayers between $63 million and $64 million.

It was not until April 1964 that the American people were told the full story of the waste and mismanagement at Sugar Grove. The details of the case were brought together by the GAO, an agency of the Congress responsible for examining government programs and auditing their costs. In a report with the matter-of-fact title "Unnecessary Costs Incurred for the Naval Radio Research Station Project at Sugar Grove, West Virginia," the GAO concluded that "the factors contributing to the spiraling estimates and costs were (1) the lack of recognition of the complexities of the Big Dish as a precision instrument and (2) the decision, based on military urgency, to proceed with construction of the Big Dish concurrently with the development of design, plans, and specifications."

In 1959, for example, the Navy was buying steel for the superstructure of Big Dish while its Bureau of Docks, which was in charge of the project, was still running masses of information through computers to determine whether the proposed designs would support the structural stresses of Big Dish. As might have been expected in an attempt to develop novel and complex forms, the computer's analysis showed, belatedly, that the plans for which steel already had been ordered would not work.

The Navy had not only started to build Big Dish before it knew whether what it was trying to construct would work;

the GAO also found that if the Navy had been carefully reviewing its operations, it would have concluded that the project should have been dropped two years before it was actually canceled by the Secretary of Defense. "We believe," said the GAO, "that the project would have been canceled earlier if a comprehensive review, similar to the one made in 1962, had been made in 1960 when the official estimate increased from about $84 million to $98 million. On the basis of the presently estimated cost of about $64 million for the project (including termination charges), we believe that such earlier cancellation would have saved a significant portion of the $52 million paid or payable after fiscal year 1960."

When Big Dish was finally canceled in 1962, it was no longer considered a top-priority defense project because by then space satellites had been developed to eavesdrop on Soviet radio transmissions. The GAO report did not mention this. Nor did it note that, as *Science* magazine pointed out in discussing the Big Dish debacle, the Navy's "desperate hurry" in trying to develop the project "may have had something to do with the Navy's desire, early in the space age, to get a piece of space jurisdiction for itself."

"Perhaps," *Science* magazine (published by the National Association for the Advancement of Science) continued in its commentary about Big Dish, "the most disturbing thing about the Sugar Grove debacle is that it apparently has not driven anyone in Washington to raving anger. Part of the reason, of course, is that McNamara—over the violent protests of the military services—has since instituted review and management procedures that would make it difficult for a similar octopus to get loose. But the principal reason for the ho-hum attitude is that when a national security tag is hung on a project, sound judgment often goes out the window."

The Navy, however, still does not like to give up sinking ships. So the admirals piped aboard the defense budget for the 1964 fiscal year a $3,830,000 authorization to turn the $64 million Big Dish disaster area into a radio receiving station for the Navy. (It always takes more money to make a defense boondoggle useful.)

Senator Robert C. Byrd of West Virginia was a willing ally in the Navy's efforts to salvage the concrete it had poured into his state's hills, and in arguing for the additional funds to convert the Sugar Grove project into a radio receiving station, the Senator appealed to the pork barrel instincts of his colleagues.

"West Virginia," Byrd told the Senate, "is at the bottom of the totem pole when it comes to defense installations, and authorizing the relocation of the radio receiving station would be a step forward in correcting this inequitable situation. For West Virginia the move would provide the state with a much needed new payroll totaling seven officers, ninety-eight enlisted men, and twenty civilian employees."

During hearings before the Senate Armed Services Committee on the Navy's plan for moving its radio receiving facilities to Sugar Grove, Byrd and Admiral Roeder, director of naval communications, conducted through questions and answers an obviously well-rehearsed Alphonse-and-Gaston act for the sake of the economic salvation of West Virginia.

So ready was Roeder with technical answers to Byrd's complicated questions that when the Admiral hesitated in response to an unexpected question from Committee Chairman Russell, the Georgia Senator commented sarcastically, "I thought you had memorized everything by heart, Admiral."

Russell also recalled that Sugar Grove was the location for "the so-called Big Dish that you people sold us several years ago." Big Dish had not been mentioned until Russell brought it up. The oversight was understandable because Congress would not be anxious to pour more money into a project that, as Russell remembered it, "the Navy sold the committees and Congress [with] great pictures flashed on a screen in the

24

highest secret session, to show you would work wonders with Big Dish."

Except for the slight rebuke administered the Navy by Senator Russell, there was no real discussion in Congress on the failure of Big Dish and the Navy's plan to spend a few more millions to salvage the Sugar Grove site. The Navy got the additional money it wanted, and the millions of dollars wasted on Big Dish have been forgotten.

Big Dish was hastily conceived and quickly put under construction. Until McNamara took a hard look at the project in 1962, Secretaries of Defense had failed to check up on it because of the head-long rush in the Pentagon toward anything that had to do with space. Members of Congress never seem to have given Big Dish a second thought because it was supposed to be justified in the name of defense.

The Army wasted $300 million on the development of a missile system that never worked because its accuracy was unreliable, its stringent maintenance requirements created serious tactical problems, and it was susceptible to electronic interference.

In a report issued in February 1964 on the Army missile, not identified by name because of national security reasons, the GAO noted that "the unsatisfactory characteristics of the weapon were known at the points in time when the Army ordered successively increasing quantities of equipment and missiles.

"The waste of program funds clearly began when," the GAO report continued, "despite knowledge that the weapon was unsuitable for tactical use, the Army bought $19 million of equipment and missiles for issue to the troops. The subsequent $84 million of procurement increased the waste to over $100 million. Moreover, other program expenditures were inconsistent with available knowledge, and a substantial but undetermined portion of the remaining costs of about $200 million was also wasted or of questionable value."

The GAO attributed this $300 million Army failure to "fundamental deficiencies in the Army's management of the program, namely the lack of effective methods for gathering and considering available and essential information, for relating such information to program objectives, and for assuring that program decisions further these objectives by specifying minimum results to be obtained."

The report, however, was hardly noticed on Capitol Hill. The lack of reaction in Congress could have been due to the inability of the GAO report to go into the details of this $300 million fiasco because of an understandable concern for national security.

The following month the GAO painstakingly recounted the way the Navy threw more than $445 million into the sea in a futile effort to develop a seaplane.

The P6M seaplane development program began in 1952 and continued over a period of seven years despite repeated failures to get the craft off the water and into the air. The Navy wanted a fast, jet-powered craft capable of laying mines and of attaining a speed of 600 knots at sea level. Navy specifications also called for a plane that could take off and land in six- to eight-foot waves, operate at altitudes up to 40,000 feet, carry a payload of 30,000 pounds, and have a range of 900 nautical miles when fully loaded. In addition, the Navy wanted the plane built so it could be easily converted to deliver special weapons, used in photographic reconnaissance work, and utilized as an in-flight refueling tanker.

For the taxpayers' $445 million, the Navy got two experimental planes, both of which crashed during tests, and six other planes called limited service or prototype craft that were still undergoing tests when the P6M program was ended in 1959. Eight other P6M production-line planes were either still undergoing tests or in various stages of production when the program ended. The Navy has claimed that it was able to salvage nearly $84 million worth of parts from the project.

"The Navy," said the GAO report on the P6M program, "spent about $209,200,000, which might have been saved, because it awarded a production contract for twenty-four operational P6M-2 seaplanes to Martin [The Glenn L. Martin Company] and entered into contracts with other contractors for facilities and supporting items when it was known that there were serious unsolved problems with the prototype aircraft.

"We found no evidence," the GAO continued, "that Navy officials had made periodic comprehensive reviews of the P6M program, wherein the deficiencies and increasing costs were evaluated in terms of the probabilities of producing a seaplane capable of accomplishing the required missions at a reasonable cost, until about May 1958, or about twenty months after the Navy had entered into the contract with the Martin Company for quantity production of operational planes."

Yet, as the Navy continued to pour money into the project, almost nothing seemed to go right for the P6M. Tests indicated it was subject to dangerous buffeting and would abruptly shift direction; that its wings were so heavy they dragged down the plane in flight; that the plane was subject to violent and uncontrollable fluctuations on water; and that it was even difficult to keep the jet engines running during takeoffs and landings because of the spray thrown up by the hull of the aircraft when it moved through water.

The GAO found that the Martin Company, the prime contractor for the P6M project, was responsible for some of the major errors that kept the program from getting off the water. "For example," said the GAO report, "after the crash of the second SP6M-1, the official Navy investigation of the crash resulted in a determination that engineering errors by Martin in translating wind tunnel measurements into the P6M configuration were basically responsible for the crash.... It cost the government more than $10 million for the design and engineering modifications needed in the six prototype YP6M-1

27

aircraft to correct the engineering errors by Martin. . . . Still another example of a deficiency which appears to reflect on the quality of Martin's performance under its P6M contracts was the placement of the jet engines on the first two experimental (XP6M-1) aircraft. The engines were so positioned that static operation of the afterburners severely scorched the skin on the sides of the hull and could be expected to create a temperature of 900 degrees Fahrenheit whereas the maximum acceptable skin temperature in this area was 250 degrees Fahrenheit."

Despite these deficiencies in its performance, Martin was not penalized because, according to the GAO, "the contract provisions, included in all three of Martin's contracts, relating to the quality of the contractor's work and the financial responsibility of the contractor therefor are one-sided in favor of the contractor and opposed to the best interests of the government.

"Even though the contractor agrees, in certain provisions, that its services will conform to high professional standards in the field," the GAO report went on to note, "these provisions are negated by other contract clauses which require the government to bear the cost correction of defects unless the defective work resulted from fraud, lack of good faith, or willful misconduct by the contractor."

The P6M contracts were what the Pentagon calls cost-plus fixed-fee agreements. Under such contracts the government promises to reimburse the contractor for all of his costs and also pay him an agreed-upon fee for his work. There are no provisions in such contracts for penalties if the contractor makes errors. "However," said the GAO in its report on the P6M contracts, "we believe that a contractor should be held financially responsible for its errors which increase the cost to the government for developmental work and production where such errors demonstrate performance that is substantially less than conformance to high professional standards in the field."

In the case of the Martin contracts, the GAO report pointed out, "even though significant deficiencies in the aircraft were determined by the Navy to be due to the contractor's errors, the contractor will not suffer any financial penalty for the cost to correct the deficiencies." The GAO also said that the Navy planned to "renegotiate the settlements of each of the three contracts with Martin in accordance with its interpretation of the terms of the contracts. In essence, this means that Martin will be reimbursed for the allowable costs, including those incurred for correction of all the defects due to Martin's errors, plus a negotiated portion of the fixed fee or guaranteed profit specified in the contract."

The errors and miscalculations that resulted in the waste of $445 million on the Navy's seaplane project were typical of what went on in the Pentagon during most of the 1950's when, in the rush to develop new weapons and better ways of delivering them, the armed services often ordered construction to proceed on an airplane or a weapon before the idea was off the drawing board.

One billion dollars was wasted on another aircraft project that never got off a drawing board. This was the atomic-powered airplane, a project continued for fifteen years.

In an exhaustive, 191-page report, issued in February 1963, on what was called the Aircraft Nuclear Propulsion (ANP) Program, jointly administered by the Defense Department and the Atomic Energy Commission, the GAO noted: "At the time of its termination, the ANP program had been redirected to the research and development stage with primary emphasis on high-performance reactors. A number of airborne reactor shielding studies had been carried out, and turbojet aircraft engines had been ground tested with nuclear energy as the heat source; however, an airplane had never been flown on nuclear power nor had a prototype airplane been built."

Difficult as the technical and scientific problems were, the Defense Department and the AEC seemed to have compounded them by frequent changes in the emphasis of the research program and by the building of facilities that were never used and in fact never needed. In the years from 1952 to 1961, when the atomic-powered airplane program was finally ended, the emphasis zigged and zagged. For thirteen months it was supposed to be a flight demonstration program, and then for the next eighteen months it was considered an applied research and development program. In November 1954 the program was turned into a weapon system, which it remained for the surprisingly long period of twenty-five months.

In January 1957, efforts were reoriented to an experimental development program with no flight objectives, but this was the objective for only two months. By April 1957, it became an experimental development program with flight objectives and remained that for ten months when it was changed—for seven months—into a development program with flight objectives as a military aircraft. It was time for a change again in October 1958 when the military usefulness of the project was once again dropped. After nine months of this, the final reorientation was made back to a research and development program leading to major reactor experiments, and there the program stayed for twenty months until it was cut off in March 1961.

"It is our view," said Herbert F. York, then the director of research and engineering for the Defense Department, in July 1959, "that during most of the past thirteen years and the expenditure of most of the $900 million [total expenditures on the program at that time], the ANP program has been characterized by attempts to find shortcuts to early flight and by brute force and expensive approaches to the problem. Thus we find that only a relatively very small fraction of the funds and energies applied to this program has gone into trying to develop a reactor with a potentially high performance.

"Most of the resources," York continued, "have been applied to attempts to develop materials which could 'fly soonest'; to develop turbine machinery; to build facilities, many of which would only be needed in support of a flight program; to conduct experiments on the radiation resistance of tires, oils, insulation, electronic components, etc.; and to develop new components. . . . As a result of this approach to the problem, we are still at least four years away from achieving flight with a reactor-engine combination . . . which can just barely fly."

Partly as a result of the frequent changes in the emphasis of the program and partly because of bad planning, a total of $17,147,000 was invested in buildings, roads, bridges, and other facilities that were never used. The GAO found expensive and unused facilities at the National Reactor Testing Station in Idaho, the Connecticut Aircraft Nuclear Engine Laboratory in Middletown, Connecticut, and the Georgia Nuclear Laboratory in Dawsonville, Georgia.

Plagued as the program was by frequent changes in direction and by decisions to build facilities before a clear need for them was established, the program also foundered because it took an incredible amount of time for decisions to be made.

"AEC [the Atomic Energy Commission] requested a major decision from DOD [Department of Defense] in December 1948," the GAO report on the nuclear airplane project noted, "but did not receive the decision until March 1951. The request concerned DOD's views on the military worth of nuclear-powered aircraft and on the urgency with which DOD regarded the proposed development program. In December 1950, AEC indicated to DOD that the need for a decision was critical from the standpoint of national defense and that a severe shortage of personnel in the atomic energy field was developing. In March 1951, AEC advised DOD that the need for a decision was particularly acute and shortly thereafter was informed by DOD of the priority to be given the aircraft nuclear power plant."

The GAO seemed to find mismanagement and waste everywhere it looked in its examination of the nuclear-powered aircraft project:

"Our review disclosed that AEC incurred unnecessary costs of about $517,000 by extending for a seven-month period a

31

contract for the processing of high-purity yttrium oxide in order to keep the production capability alive. Placing the production facility in a standby condition would have accomplished the same purpose, and the contractor was willing to negotiate to keep the production capability alive. . . .

"Our review disclosed that a delay in AEC's and GE's [The General Electric Company] agreeing on an indemnity provision in the contract may have resulted in delays in certain contractor personnel. There was a delay of about eighteen months in initiating work on critical experiments because, although GE employees had been trained and were prepared to proceed on critical experiments in December 1952, the experiments were not started until about July 1954. We understand that such experiments were necessary and should have been carried out concurrently with the development of the reactor. . . .

"In one instance, work covered by large negotiated contract modifications was almost entirely subcontracted and in turn sub-subcontracted, resulting in a pyramiding of overhead and profit allowances totaling over $237,000 to the prime contractor and the subcontractor for work done principally by the sub-subcontractor. We believe that a substantial portion of such overhead and profit allowances was unnecessary and could have been avoided had the Corps of Engineers (1) obtained competitive proposals from firms able to provide the required construction services or (2) taken steps to eliminate use of the tiers involved in the successive subcontracting."

So disorganized and full of waste was the nuclear plane project that the Joint Congressional Committee on Atomic Energy, an advocate of the program, was moved in February 1959, after a series of hearings into the project, to issue this eight-point criticism of it:

"1. The program still has no firm set of objectives looking toward the development of a nuclear propelled aircraft;

"2. No decision has been made regarding actual nuclear flight and no target dates have been set for such flight;

"3. Recommendation of the project director as to funding levels required to get the job done have been virtually ignored;

"4. It is authoritatively estimated that cuts in proposed funding levels for the program in fiscal 1960 will delay the achievement of a ground test prototype for an additional year and will thereby delay achievement of nuclear flight for at least that period of time;

"5. Administrative indecision at high levels and inter-service rivalries have plagued the program from the start and have rendered a great disservice to the nation;

"6. No less than seven advisory committees have been set up in the past decade to review the program, including the so-called Killian Committee, and yet the contractors in the field still have no clear guidance as to where they stand or where the program is going;

"7. The annual expenditure of $150 million for the ANP program as a holding operation to avoid difficult technical and administrative decisions which must be made to lend clear-cut direction to the program is a completely indefensible use of the taxpayers' money;

"8. The Air Force and the Navy, after due consideration by their expert military advisers, have established firm requirements for nuclear-propelled aircraft. The Air Force and the AEC both recommended an increase in their own fiscal 1960 budgets for the program to back up these requirements, but have been turned down."

Complaints such as those made in 1959 by the Joint Committee on Atomic Energy were rarely heard on Capitol Hill, however, throughout the fifteen-year, billion dollar nuclear aircraft debacle. Nor were there any outraged cries on the floors of the Senate and the House when in the winter of 1963 the GAO issued its fully documented report on the waste of a billion dollars in the name of defense.

Secretary McNamara has attributed much of the waste in military spending to this penchant in the Pentagon for bending metal into weapons and machinery before workable plans have left the drawing boards of scientists and engineers. Another reason for the wasting of money on airplanes that never fly or other projects that fail to materialize is the intense competition among the three services for the defense dollar.

"All too often," McNamara told the Senate-House Subcommittee on Defense Procurement in March 1963, "large-scale weapons systems developments, and even production programs, have been undertaken before we had clearly defined what was wanted and before we had clearly determined that there existed a suitable technological base on which to draw in developing a system.

"And all too often," McNamara added, "insufficient attention has been paid to how a proposed weapons system would be used, what it would cost, and, finally, whether the contribution the weapon could make to our military capability would be worth the cost. . . .

"Prior planning and even feasibility testing of 'pacing' components are a lot cheaper than having to reorient, stretch out, or terminate expensive projects after they have been started. There are, of course, exceptions to this general rule. Where a development can add a new and unique dimension to our military capability, like the A and H bombs and the ICBM, great costs and risk are justified. But such cases are rare. The typical development promises, if successful, to achieve a capability that can also be achieved in other ways or represents an improvement of but modest proportions in our total military capability.

"In these cases the urgency is not as great and the employment of a more measured and orderly approach to development and production is fully justified. In fact, I have observed that in most cases careful and comprehensive prior planning actually saves time as well as money and results in more effective and more dependable weapons."

Nevertheless, a total of $3.7 billion was spent by the Air Force on an attack warning system that was obsolete before it was completed. The system was called SAGE (Semi-Automatic Ground Environment). It consisted of twenty-two centers filled with extremely expensive radio and computer equipment, and it was sold to Congress as a sophisticated radar apparatus that would use computers to give instant warnings in the event of the approach of Soviet bombers. The only trouble with SAGE was that as late as 1964 it was not completely operational, and this of course is now the missile age rather than the day of the bomber.

"The great problem," Secretary McNamara pointed out in testimony in 1963 before the House Defense Appropriations subcommittee, "is that in a missile age we must assume they will first attack with missiles before their bombers attack; and almost certainly among the targets for their missile attack would be our SAGE centers, in which case they would be out of operation before the bombers arrive, and unless we had a backup system to substitute for those SAGE centers that were destroyed we would not be able to properly control the interceptors at the time of the bomber attack."

So, McNamara explained, the Defense Department was asking Congress to appropriate more millions for what the Pentagon calls its BUIC, a semiautomatic Back-Up Interceptor Control. Before McNamara could spread out before the congressmen the wonders of his own BUIC, Representative Daniel J. Flood, a Democrat from Pennsylvania, wanted to have, and did, a final word on SAGE.

"I went out of my way hour after hour," said Flood, "to bet somebody else a hat that this pigeon would be obsolete before it was operational, and I had no takers."

As McNamara has conceded several times in testimony before congressional committees, the trouble with the SAGE centers is that they are all above ground and would be extremely vulnerable to air attack. The Russians would surely direct part of an early missile attack on the SAGE centers, the locations

35

of which are well known. Yet the cost of hardening the SAGE sites to protect them against Soviet attacks would be prohibitively expensive.

So, for the last three years the Defense Department has been building BUIC to provide a backup for the SAGE centers, most of which probably would be knocked out during a Soviet attack. The BUIC centers will be far more widely dispersed than are the SAGE installations and, it is hoped, will be all but impregnable to a missile or bomber raid.

"For the trans-attack and post-attack periods," McNamara has said, "the SAGE system alone would be of questionable value because of its concentration and vulnerability. The presently planned number of SAGE direction centers backed up by the BUIC stations, however, will present a much more viable system, since the BUIC stations will be widely dispersed away from other prime targets and would not offer very profitable targets for ICBM attack. Furthermore, the crews will be provided with fallout protection needed to enable them to function in the postmissile attack environment. The phaseout of the additional SAGE direction centers when BUIC becomes operational will, together with the six previously phased out, produce a total savings of $82 million per year."

So out of date is SAGE that the Federal Aviation Agency has repeatedly turned down persistent efforts by the Air Force to get it to take over many of the units in the system and use them to help control civilian air traffic. Former FAA Administrator Najeeb E. Halaby believed air passengers deserved something better than SAGE and let the Air Force know that the FAA was not in the business of providing civilian parachutes for military white elephants.

The kind of waste that Congress tolerates in the Pentagon makes the mistakes in such heavily-criticized programs as foreign aid and farm subsidies seem miniscule. Yet, congressional committees have never investigated such Pentagon blunders as the Big Dish, the missile that refused to be guided, the P6M seaplane that would not fly, the nuclear-powered plane that never got off the drawing boards, and the radar warning system that was obsolete before it was completed.

"Congress, of course, has a deep responsibility for the economic strength of our country," Admiral Hyman G. Rickover has commented in discussing these problems with the House Defense Appropriations subcommittee. "Individual senators and congressmen also have a responsibility to their own states and districts. However, I do believe it is harmful to our country for the military establishment to be used as a vehicle for correcting economic problems and inequalities. For example, there have been shipbuilding contracts awarded over a period of several years to a shipbuilder at considerably higher prices than the going rate at other yards. From a political standpoint it may have been worthwhile to pay more to keep the shipbuilder in that area in business. From a military standpoint it resulted in a reduction in the number of ships the Navy could buy. Perhaps if we continue procedures such as this we should openly earmark the extra cost as a subsidy, and not charge it to the military.

"Although I can understand the desire to obtain as much federal funds as possible for a given state or district," Rickover went on to say, "I do not believe this is a permanent solution to the unemployment problem. In fact it may ultimately make the problem worse. A large project assigned to a locality may attract many unemployed from other areas. There is then the permanent problem of keeping all the people, the old ones as well as the newcomers, employed—and this means constantly fighting for new and more contracts in the future.

"In recent years," Rickover noted, "Secretaries of Defense have attempted with more or less success to close down excess defense installations. I believe this effort should be fully supported or we will not be able to have the efficient defense establishment we must have to survive. If economics is to be the handmaiden of politics, the worst place for it is in our defense. There are many other places where it does little or no harm. Several years ago a Secretary of the Navy told me he estimated that to keep a certain nonessential activity in operation was costing about $10,000 a vote."

As Rickover knows so well, politics has become the handmaiden of defense, from the White House down through the Pentagon and the committees on Capitol Hill to each congressional district. No one, not even as strong a secretary of defense as McNamara, has been able to move the Pentagon out of politics.

CHAPTER 3

Contracts—the Politician's Role

PRESIDENT JOHNSON began a political tour of California on a pleasant June day in 1964 by stopping at the 300,000 acre Edwards Air Force Base in the Mojave Desert. The President used the occasion to remind Californians of the bounties the defense program had brought to their state. He pointed out that California had been awarded $21 billion worth of defense contracts since President Kennedy was inaugurated in 1961. Johnson also noted that California "is responsible for 23.1 percent of the entire defense effort—more than twice as much as its nearest competitor" and that "defense personnel in this state represent an annual payroll of almost $2 billion a year—half a billion more than in 1960."

Over thirty years of experience on Capitol Hill conditioned Johnson to look on government contracts, whether for rivers and harbors projects or for missiles, as useful political tools. In a speech in Dallas in April 1963, when he was Vice President, Johnson said that "our space program is creating and helping create new basic industries for our economy" and pointed out that "the number of private companies and space research organizations participating in our space programs has grown in

39

less than six years to more than five thousand." Johnson, whose duties as Vice President included the chairmanship of the National Aeronautics and Space Council, went on to say that the space program not only was helping the economy of Texas but also had "brought about a major rejuvenation to New England . . . is generating new growth and prosperity in the Deep South and Southeast, and will be an increasingly important source of contracts and jobs in economic activity for the Great Lakes, the Northwest, and the Rocky Mountain states."

Johnson's Texas has indeed benefited from both the space and defense programs. In 1961 the $160 million Manned Spacecraft Center of the National Aeronautics and Space Administration was located near Houston. The Center employs 3,500 people and has attracted satellite installations maintained by space contractors who want to be nearby. And it is more than coincidental that the center is in the congressional district of Representative Albert Thomas, who is chairman of the House Appropriations subcommittee that reviews the NASA budget each year. Texas also got, in 1962, the largest contract ever awarded for a defense program—the controversial $6.5 billion TFX airplane project. The plane will be built by General Dynamics Corporation, a Texas-based firm, and much of the work will be done at the company's plant in Fort Worth.

But Johnson was not the first President to put defense contracts into a political campaign. President Kennedy injected the politics of defense-contract awards into the 1962 congressional campaign when he spoke in West Virginia and Pennsylvania. He pointed with pride to the increasing number of defense contracts that his Administration had put into both states and told a Pennsylvania audience that "working with Governor Lawrence since 1960, we have increased by 50 percent the number of prime defense contracts that come to Pennsylvania."

Kennedy may have provided a precedent for Johnson's use of defense contracts as a presidential political issue, but Johnson went considerably further in the exploitation of the issue in 1964 than Kennedy did in the two years and ten months he was in office. Three times in 1964 Johnson used a supersonic plane originally called the A-11 to ward off political criticism of his Administration's opposition to the further development of manned bombers. Johnson revealed the existence of the A-11 in March when he told a press conference that the plane could fly more than 2,000 miles an hour at altitudes above 70,000 feet. At that time the Administration was trying to fight off efforts in Congress to accelerate plans and tests that would culminate in the construction of a supersonic bomber along the lines of the proposed B-70 (later renamed the RS-70) that Secretary of Defense McNamara had decided was not needed. The A-11 was presented to the public not only as the answer to the big-bomber advocates but also as a reply to such critics of the Administration's emphasis on missiles as Senator Barry Goldwater of Arizona, the Republican presidential nominee. It was just nine days after Goldwater's nomination that the A-11 was unveiled again, this time in the guise of the SR-11 strategic reconnaissance system. Voters last heard of the A-11 on September 30 when, rechristened again, this time as the YF-12A, the plane was put on public display for the press to view.

McNamara may be an efficient Secretary of Defense who for the first time since World War II asserted civilian supremacy over military programs but, to his discredit, McNamara also thrust himself deeply into partisan politics. He became the first Secretary of Defense to testify before a committee drafting a party platform. Ironically, McNamara was considered a Republican when President Kennedy chose him as his Secretary of Defense.

"The Defense Department we found in 1961 was one in which each military service made its own independent plans," McNamara told the Democratic Platform Committee in August 1964. "We found the Army relying on airlift which the Air Force was unable to provide. We found the Army envisioning a long war, stockpiling supplies for as long as two years; while the Air Force, envisioning a short war, had supplies for only a few days. We found a weapons inventory completely lacking in certain major elements required for combat readiness. . . . In 1961, we found military strategy to be the stepchild of a predetermined budget."

McNamara failed to mention that he had also found the "missile gap," a Kennedy issue in the 1960 campaign, to be non-existent, a fact the Secretary had blurted out to the press early in 1961 before he became an accomplished spokesman in behalf of his adopted party's political objectives. McNamara did, however, spell out to the Platform Committee what he considered his accomplishments as Secretary of Defense, and they are many.

The Secretary's political performance did not escape some scathing criticism from his immediate predecessor, Thomas S. Gates, President Eisenhower's last Secretary of Defense. In a letter to McNamara in September 1964, Gates noted that the Secretary had "often given me and the Eisenhower Administration great credit for having provided a proper background and framework" for present policies and that McNamara took office "in what I think we have agreed was an orderly and fruitful transition."

"I agree completely," Gates continued in his letter to McNamara, "that the national interest and the credibility of our defense posture require the Secretary of Defense to speak out. I would not have chosen the forum of a national political platform committee to do this; but even in that forum, it would have been possible to defend Administration policies affirmatively and aggressively without making charges against those who preceded you and did their best to insure the nation's security, and whose efforts you earlier had found frequent occasion to commend."

During 1964 both of the vice presidential candidates, Democratic Senator Hubert H. Humphrey of Minnesota and Republican Representative William E. Miller of New York, involved themselves in the politics of defense contracts and the closely-allied space program. When Humphrey was campaigning in early October in Seattle, the home of the Boeing Company, he announced that the Johnson Administration would try to expand the export market for American airplanes by making loans fully competitive with those granted by European countries.

From a political standpoint, Humphrey could not have chosen a better place than Seattle to make this announcement. Less than two years earlier, Boeing, which employs fifty thousand persons in the Seattle area, had lost out when the huge TFX contract was awarded to General Dynamics. Since then Boeing had also lost business to the French Caravelle aircraft because of the generous credit terms extended to purchasers of the plane by the French government. By announcing the credit-terms plans in Seattle, Humphrey also made it possible for Democratic Senator Henry M. Jackson of Washington, who was reelected in 1964 despite Boeing's government-contract problems, to bask in the political glow of such a pledge of assistance to the American aircraft industry.

Later in October, Representative Miller told an audience in Marietta, Georgia, where the Lockheed Aircraft Corporation produces C-131 and C-140 jet cargo transports for the Air Force, that there was "rampant politics" in the defense program under President Johnson but that "you won't have to worry about economic conditions in this area" because "we [Republicans] don't believe in sole reliance on the ballistic missile."

While Miller was promising Georgians that the Republicans would provide even more jobs in defense plants than had the Democrats, across the country in California the same question was becoming a major issue in that state's closely-contested senatorial campaign where Republican George Murphy defeated Democrat Pierre Salinger by a slight margin.

After touring California's Vandenberg Air Force Base in mid-September Murphy issued a statement saying: "It is time California was told the whole truth about future prospects for

43

California's defense industry. California's economic health, particularly employment, is seriously threatened by Defense Department plans to drastically cut procurement appropriations. Appropriations in the federal defense procurement budget are down $1.8 billion from last year. . . . Unemployment in California is already 6 percent of the work force. What will happen if defense spending is reduced further? Are California's workers just to be laid off by the thousands without notice or planning?"

Ten days later Murphy issued another statement: "The day of reckoning for California's immense defense industry is rapidly approaching. . . . It is time Mr. Salinger explained just where he stands on Administration plans to reduce California's share of defense contracts. He should also speak up on whether he agrees or disagrees that too many contracts are going to the President's home state of Texas. Silent Salinger cannot sit out an issue which involves one out of every ten industrial jobs in California. California has to speak up for its share of defense dollars or we're going to let Massachusetts, Texas, New York, and other states grab off contracts which we must have to keep our people employed. California employment figures for August showed a 6.5 percent drop in the aerospace and defense work force. More than 33,000 workers have lost their jobs in ballistics, electronics, and aircraft industries in the past year. . . . Mr. Salinger claims he knows the 'right people' to see in Washington to get California defense contracts. Does Mr. Salinger mean that he is going to sit down with a group of officials and make political deals with our defense budget? California wants no part of backroom deals. . . . We have more highly-trained personnel, more scientific resources, and more know-how than any other state. In a fair and open competition on merits for defense contracts, we will once again receive our fair share of business."

On the one hand Murphy seemed to be saying that his election would automatically bring more defense contracts to California. On the other hand, he was openly criticizing Salinger for indicating that he had enough special connections in Washington to get contracts other than through competitive bidding.

Representative Charles H. Wilson, a freshman Democratic congressman from Los Angeles, replied on Salinger's behalf with a speech entitled "Republicans Endanger California Jobs" delivered in the House of Representatives late in September. It was a speech of the kind that fills out so many issues of the *Congressional Record* as election time approaches—a speech designed to be reprinted in pamphlet form for the folks back home.

"Members of the Republican Party, in the most cynical way possible," Wilson began, "are attempting to perpetrate a hoax and fiction on the people of California by confusing and distorting the employment picture in my state. On the one hand, we find Republican candidates demanding that more jobs be brought to the West Coast and on the other hand we find California Republicans in this House voting against the bills which are the very lifeblood of federal job opportunities in my state. . . . In fiscal year 1963 the National Aeronautics and Space Administration placed almost $2 billion in contracts and procurement orders with California companies. This high figure is in fact 50.4 percent of all the business done by NASA during this period. To demonstrate how massive is California's share of NASA contract awards we need only see that the second-placed state in receipt of NASA contracts received only 9 percent of the total business for the year. . . . I wonder just how our Republican candidates plan to improve upon this figure. In the nonspace field, California also leads the nation in the number and amount of Department of Defense contracts and procurement awards received. During fiscal year 1963 approximately 25 percent of all Defense Department orders came to California, and no other state in the country receives anywhere close to this much business. . . . Any candidate for public office who makes the claim he can bring more federal work to California or who claims that the Democratic Party has not done enough

45

for California is either ignorant of the true situation or is deliberately attempting to mislead and confuse the people."

So went the argument about who could get the biggest piece of the defense pie for California, an argument the Republican won. In another western state, Utah, a similar argument was won by a Democrat. Utah's Democratic senator, Frank E. Moss, was challenged in 1964 by Ernest B. Wilkinson, a former president of Brigham Young University. Wilkinson kept reminding Utah voters that the state had lost nearly six thousand jobs in its missile industry—one third of the total—in just eighteen months and that Utah would get only four-thousandths of 1 percent of the $5.3 billion NASA budget for the 1965 fiscal year.

"This year, then," Republican Senator Wallace E. Bennett of Utah said in a Senate speech reinforcing Wilkinson's argument, "Utah will receive a mere twenty cents per person from the space budget. Contrast this to Texas which will get $250 million, or $25 per person along with a new space center at Houston. California, even with its great population, will receive $143 per person."

Bennett argued that these figures showed a Democratic senator has considerably less influence with his own Administration in the awarding of defense contracts than is generally supposed, and back in Utah candidate Wilkinson maintained that he could get more contracts than Moss, who was busy explaining that the state's missile industry was declining because the nation was catching up with its defense needs.

In Wyoming, liberal Democratic Senator Gale McGee was also reelected following a campaign in which he stressed the number of missile bases and other defense installations his state obtained during his six years in the Senate. Not surprisingly, McGee claimed credit for all of them.

The possibility of disarmament and the realities of constant changes in arms production were also an issue in Wyoming and Utah, as well as in New Mexico and Idaho during the 1964 campaign. The disarmament issue was brought into western politics as a result of campaign contributions from members of an organization called the Council for a Livable World, founded in 1962 by the nuclear physicist Leo Szilard, who died in June 1964. Szilard conceived of the council, which claimed a membership of 2,500 in 1964, as a political force to help bring about worldwide disarmament. He decided that the way to do this was to help elect senators who would work for the council's disarmament goals.

In 1962 the members of the council contributed funds to seven senatorial candidates. Their greatest success was in South Dakota where Senator McGovern received $22,000 from the council. This amounted to a fourth of his total campaign funds, and McGovern, who won by only 597 votes, conceded that he probably could not have been elected without the money raised by the council.

In 1964 the members of the council concentrated on helping Moss, McGee, Democratic Representative Joseph Montoya, who was elected to the Senate from New Mexico, and Democratic Representative Ralph R. Harding of Idaho, who was defeated. The council was interested in helping reelect Harding to the House because he planned to run for the Senate in 1966. Democratic Senator Quentin N. Burdick of North Dakota was also on the council's list for financial help in 1964, but after the council was sharply criticized by conservative Western Republicans like Senator Milward Simpson of Wyoming and Senator Peter Dominick of Colorado, Burdick returned to the council $14,000 contributed to his campaign by its members.

In a statement Simpson placed in the *Congressional Record* in October 1964, the Council for a Livable World was called "a secret political organization with a satchel full of money" and was accused of advocating "unilateral disarmament, stripping the United States of its muscle, [and] turning the country into a fourth-rate power at the mercy of the international wolf-pack." The statement also charged that the council was deliberately concentrating its efforts in thinly populated states "where a political buck packs a bigger punch."

The council, most of whose members are scientists, scholars, and educators, has never advocated unilateral disarmament. Its work had been praised by President Johnson, who expressed the hope at the time of Szilard's death that the council would carry on his efforts to help maintain world peace. But the defense program means badly needed jobs in the western states; so disarmament can easily be turned into a fighting political word.

Meanwhile, back east in New York, defense contracts were also a major issue in the Senate race between Republican Senator Kenneth B. Keating and former Attorney General Robert F. Kennedy, a contest Kennedy won. Here the politicians of both parties were promising to do everything possible to keep open the New York Naval Shipyard in Brooklyn. Since 1952 employment in the installation, which has facilities to build as well as repair ships, had declined by more than 50 percent, but the 9,700 workers who remained still constituted, along with their families and friends, a formidable political block. At meetings with the Navy yard workers, both Keating and Kennedy said they would come to the aid of the men. Two days after the election the victor Kennedy and the vanquished Keating joined forces to meet with Secretary McNamara to plead for the retention if not the expansion of the venerable but outmoded yard. The Brooklyn facility was one of three Navy yards ordered closed by McNamara three weeks after the 1964 elections, a decision bitterly protested by New York politicians. There is little doubt, however, that if McNamara could have had his nonpolitical way, the inefficient Navy yards would have been terminated much sooner than they were.

Defense-contract politics has increasingly figured in state and national election campaigns as the defense program has become an accepted and expected part of the American economy. In 1962, for example, Democratic Representative David King

48

of Utah made many hand-shaking tours of industrial plants in his unsuccessful campaign to unseat Senator Bennett. Before shaking hands with the workers on the assembly lines, King spent a few minutes with the plant managers. He let them know that he knew President Kennedy well, was in and out of the White House a lot, had frequent telephone conversations with the President, and would be in a position in the Senate to help the managers with their defense contract problems.

In Michigan the day before the 1962 elections, Democratic Governor John Swainson hurriedly called a press conference to announce that a $100 million missile contract had been awarded to a Texas company that had agreed to do the work in an idle Detroit factory. The news had been given to Swainson by Michigan's Democratic Senator Philip Hart, who had been accorded an election-eve break on it by the White House. The next morning on their way to the polls, voters saw headlines such as this one in the Detroit *Free Press:* "100 Million Missile Deal to Make 5,000 Jobs Here." But Swainson apparently needed more than a missile contract. He was defeated by George Romney.

In 1960 when President Eisenhower was still in office, his Administration set up an informal clearing committee to keep Republican members of Congress advised well in advance of plans that might result in the closing of defense plants and military installations before the presidential elections that year. The members of the committee included Vice President Richard M. Nixon, Senator Thruston B. Morton of Kentucky, who was then chairman of the Republican National Committee, and representatives from the White House staff, the Bureau of the Budget, and the Department of Defense.

"In the last Congress," Morton said in explaining the clearing committee to a reporter, "I spent a lot of time and effort trying to persuade two Republican members of the House, who come from labor districts, to support the Administration's labor legislation. One of them flatly refused, saying it would be political suicide. The other finally reluctantly agreed to go along with us. The very next day the Pentagon announced without the slightest previous warning that a big base would be shut down in the district of the House member I had laboriously won over. But that isn't all. In that same announcement, the Pentagon also said that a new installation would be built in the other member's district: the one who had turned me down because he feared it would be political suicide for him to vote with us. I had a tough time straightening that 'snafu' out, and I don't want any more of them. That's why we simply must have a 'clearing committee' to keep a checkrein on these things."

Defense-contract politics is not just a campaign-time gambit, however. It is a game played the year round, and senators and representatives have staff members who are constantly trying to put pressure on the Pentagon to get more contracts for constituents. "In the first place," Democratic Senator William Proxmire of Wisconsin has said, "the huge defense industry constitutes a devastatingly effective lobby in working on both the executive and the legislative branch of government. In every state and in almost every congressional district, labor, public officials, and management combine to convert many a congressman into a fighting advocate of more military contracts. . . . The heaviest lobbying pressure—and the most potent with Congress—is to hold on to old weapons, keep old assembly lines rolling, and maintain old jobs. . . . The Army, Navy, and Air Force quietly and skillfully lobby congressmen daily in what must be the most all-encompassing lobby operation in history, with more than five hundred Pentagon lobbyists, euphoniously called legislative liaison men, attending members of Congress. There is now one armed forces lobbyist for every member of Congress." At the end of World War II, Proxmire pointed out, the military had only five legislative agents on Capitol Hill.

One of the major jobs of the military lobbyists is to make sure that members of Congress belonging to the party in the

White House can reap every political benefit from each defense contract in their state or district. Almost every weekday morning a Pentagon messenger takes to the White House a list of defense contract awards to be made public. Presidential aides telephone the glad tidings to Democratic members of Congress from the states or districts where the work will be done and military officers from the Pentagon bring copies of the contract announcements to Capitol Hill. The senators and representatives in turn telephone the news to newspapers and radio and television stations back home. That night voters read or hear that Senator X or Congressman Y announced the award of a defense contract that will mean more jobs for their community. During the Eisenhower years from 1953 to 1961, Republicans were given the same opportunity to take all of the credit for defense contracts.

Most of the contract awards announced by members of Congress were made on the basis of competitive bidding, design competition, or other routine Pentagon procedures. Sometimes a senator or representative does not even know a firm in his state or district has been seeking a contract. Republican Representative Charles McC. Mathias, Jr., of Maryland summed up the procedure when he told the House in 1963: "It's a confidence game in which the people's money is used to bamboozle them on a national scale into thinking their Democratic congressmen are performing great feats." Mathias was angry because the announcement of a contract award to a company he had been trying to help for two years was made by Democratic Representative Carlton R. Sickles, Maryland's congressman-at-large. What is more, the announcement was held up until Sickles could have his picture taken congratulating the president of the company.

Republican Senator Margaret Chase Smith of Maine, a member of the Senate Armed Services Committee and a retired member of the Air Force reserve, has called the contract-announcement game "a Keystone Kops comedy" in which admirals are cast in "degrading messenger boy roles, delivering to Capitol Hill Republicans messages that have already been delivered hours or days before to the favored Democratic Senators or congressmen—and even already announced by the favored Democrats." Mrs. Smith was incensed because her junior colleague, Democratic Senator Edmund Muskie, was given information on contract awards before she was—even though she was a ranking Republican member of the Senate Armed Services Committee.

After Democrat Edward M. (Ted) Kennedy was elected to the Senate from Massachusetts in November 1962, Republican members of Congress from the state complained that every contract award was announced by him so it looked to Massachusetts voters as if Kennedy, who campaigned on the slogan "He Can Do More for Massachusetts," had won for the state a hundred million dollars worth of defense contracts within a month of his election. Republican Representative Silvio O. Conte of Massachusetts said that he once received a contract announcement with a note saying: "You have a four-day lead on this story." But when members of his staff telephoned the news to newspapers and radio and television stations back home, they discovered that Senator Kennedy had announced the contract the day before.

Less than a month before Ted Kennedy was elected, the White House intervened to prevent the closing of M-14 rifle production lines in a factory in Worcester, Massachusetts, and M-14 rifle production in the state was not ended until 1963.

In December 1962, even before he had been sworn in as a senator, young Kennedy went to the Grumman Aircraft offices on Long Island to carry out his campaign promise "to visit industries throughout the country and to promote the skills and training of Massachusetts labor and to encourage industries wherever possible to locate plants" in his state. Grumman has a $1.5 billion contract for construction of the lunar excursion module or "bug" to be used in landing a man on the moon.

Kennedy wanted to get some of the work subcontracted to Massachusetts electronics firms. "On the part of most newly elected Senators such tactics would have little effect," Kenneth B. Keating, who was then a Republican senator from New York, said in criticizing Kennedy's unusual visit. "On the part of the President's brother, they constitute a strong and subtle form of pressure which may well be widely resented throughout New York and other states."

Whatever resentment Kennedy's visit may have caused elsewhere, it got Massachusetts more government business. In July 1963 Kennedy announced that a $50 million subcontract had been awarded by Grumman to an RCA plant in Massachusetts.

Representative Gerald R. Ford, Jr., of Michigan, the senior Republican member on the House Appropriations subcommittee that handles the defense budget before he became House Republican leader in 1965, discovered he always got notices of contract awards, sometimes delivered to his office by commissioned officers, just a little too late to meet the deadlines of the afternoon papers in his district. But, Ford said, Michigan's two Democratic senators were given the announcements in plenty of time.

The use of commissioned officers as Capitol Hill messenger boys became so flagrant in 1963 that Republican Senator John J. Williams of Delaware protested in a letter to Secretary McNamara: "Unless this political farce is checked . . . I am afraid it will develop into the greatest era of influence peddling we have ever seen."

Williams cited the case of a defense contract awarded to a company in a state where both senators and the representative in whose district the firm was located were "all very friendly with the Administration."

"Therefore," Williams said, "three high-ranking officers were dispatched to the Capitol with a notification for each of the three members. To make sure that there was no partiality shown, the officers even synchronized their watches and by prearranged plan entered the offices of their designated congressional member on the exact minute. All of these precautions and the utilization of the services of these three officers were being taken to allow some members of Congress to claim credit for something with which they had nothing to do; in fact, in this instance not one of them even knew that the company in question was bidding on the contract."

Williams also said: "One dangerous aspect of the policy is the tendency of national or state political organizations to capitalize on the influence their candidates will have in Washington as an excuse to collect larger political contributions from these defense contractors. . . . Defense contractors in some states are now being openly told that the easiest way to get government contracts is to elect as their representatives in Congress men who have the closest ties or relationships with the Administration."

McNamara and his aides have dismissed this system, which began under Eisenhower but was institutionalized by Kennedy and Johnson, as a relatively harmless political charade. Most senators and representatives defend it as part of the game of politics. "Credit-taking is the lifeblood of politics," one member of Congress said in commenting on the system. "Do you want to drain us of our lifeblood?"

In replying to the letter from Williams, McNamara said that "this practice of advance notification is one of long standing and predates my tenure in office" and that he would continue the practice.

"One of the traditional complaints of Congress vis-à-vis the executive branch," McNamara continued in his defense of the contract-notification system, "is that Congress is not kept adequately informed. And so our policy has been to provide members of Congress, as a matter of courtesy and to the extent feasible, with relevant information about our activities, whether that information be favorable (e.g., contract awards), or unfavorable (e.g., base closures, reduction in force, etc.) from a particular individual's point of view."

McNamara denied that Democrats were favored in the release of contract information, but he did promise Williams that commissioned officers would no longer be used to deliver the contract messages on Capitol Hill.

Political sophisticates in Washington may know that Democratic members of Congress often take credit for contracts that were negotiated without their assistance, but businessmen back home do not necessarily know this. They are constantly writing to their senators and representatives to enlist their aid. A letter or telephone call from a member of Congress, in turn, does not always change a military bureaucrat's mind, but at the very least such calls cause the services to take another look at a contract to see if it could be swung the interested congressman's way.

By letting Democratic members of Congress announce the awarding of contracts, President Johnson and Secretary McNamara have cast a political pall over the entire defense program. Many businessmen would like to stop the system, and the United States Chamber of Commerce approved a resolution at its annual meeting in 1963 calling for an end to it. But there are no signs that Johnson wants to give up the political advantages in the system any more than did Kennedy or Eisenhower.

So, the route taken by defense contractors in their efforts to exercise influence in Washington is quite obvious. The contractors are, for example, usually generous contributors to hundred-dollar-a-plate political fund-raising dinners. In the spring of 1963, J. B. (Jack) Rettaliata, a vice-president of Grumman Aircraft Engineering Corporation, was one of the organizers of a $180,000 Democratic dinner on Long Island. Grumman is both a space and defense contractor. In sending out invitations for the dinner to four hundred of Grumman's suppliers and subcontractors, Rettaliata noted that a program was being published in connection with the dinner and said that taking an advertisement in the program "will excuse any obligation."

Even more serious, however, are the political and economic pressures that the services and their contractors generate in Congress for the development of weapons or the continuance of programs of marginal value. Often the services are genuinely convinced that the weapons are needed, but sometimes projects are promoted merely to increase the prestige and power of the Air Force, the Army, or the Navy.

In 1963 pressure of this kind temporarily saved a proposed Air Force weapon called the MMRBM, a mobile medium-range ballistic missile that would have been mounted on a huge trailer truck and hurled at an enemy from 500 to 1,500 miles away. The MMRBM weapons would have been used in Western Europe where they presumably would have been constantly in range of Soviet military installations. McNamara had never been more than lukewarm toward the weapon because he felt it would largely duplicate the Navy's Polaris missile, but the MMRBM always had the strong support of the Joint Chiefs of Staff.

McNamara did include $143 million in the defense budget for the 1964 fiscal year for the development of the MMRBM. Looking for places to make token reductions in defense spending, the House Appropriations Committee cut the MMRBM funds to $43 million and the House sustained the committee's action. When the defense bill got to the Senate Appropriations Committee, McNamara decided that the vanishing $100 million was not worth fighting for, but the Air Force donned its Capitol Hill battle dress and enlisted the MMRBM contractors in a Senate skirmish to save the weapon.

Fortunately for the Air Force, much of the work on the MMRBM would have been done in Arizona, the home of eighty-seven-year-old Democratic Senator Carl Hayden, who is chairman of the Senate Appropriations Committee. In the fifty-three years Hayden has served in Congress, he has become a legend in his state largely because of his extraordinary ability to get federal money and projects for Arizona, so it did not take much persuasion on the part of the MMRBM contractors to convince the Senator of the political and economic value to his state of the new weapon. Hughes Aircraft, which would have assembled the missiles in its plant in Tucson, and Goodyear Aircraft, which would have built the trailers in Phoenix, immediately went to work not only on Hayden but also on Arizona Senator Goldwater, who as a general in the Air Force reserve was one of the service's most active supporters on Capitol Hill.

Charts extolling the MMRBM were spread before the Arizona delegation. The state's senators and representatives were bombarded with telegrams from chambers of commerce back home reminding them of all the jobs the MMRBM would create in Arizona. Hughes Aircraft was also busy lobbying the California congressional delegation, as was Ford's Aeronautical Division. Both Hughes and Ford would do some of the work on the MMRBM in California. Other contractors were at work elsewhere. Thiokol, a Pennsylvania firm, would carry out its part of the project at its facilities in Utah. General Precision would bring MMRBM jobs to New York as well as to New Jersey.

In a typical thirty-minute presentation of the case for MMRBM by one contractor, the first ten minutes were taken up with a glowing statement of the importance of the weapon to the defense of the free world. The next twenty minutes were devoted to a description of the economic benefits that production of the MMRBM would bring to the senator's state. The senator was shown an elaborate chart outlining the number of jobs that would be created as production built up each year. Why, the enthusiastic contractor said, this might even

57

mean the establishment of a whole new town in your state! The presentation ended with the contractor reminding the senator that he had contributed money to his last campaign and was looking forward to working with him again.

The 1963 MMRBM campaign succeeded. The Senate Appropriations Committee voted $103 million for the project, $60 million more than the House had allowed it. When Senator Proxmire tried on the Senate floor to delete the additional money, Senator Moss of Utah quickly came to the MMRBM's defense, though he neglected to mention that the weapon would mean jobs for his state. The $103 million for the MMRBM stayed in the Senate bill, and the measure emerged from a Senate-House conference with a final appropriation of $73 million for the project.

By the summer of 1964, however, the MMRBM was in trouble again. In the budget for the 1965 fiscal year, McNamara sought $110 million for the weapon, but this time, the appropriation was cut back by Congress to $40 million.

Late in August 1964, the Pentagon announced that work on the MMRBM was being stopped, after two futile, frustrating years that had cost taxpayers $100 million for a weapon that never defended anyone or anything.

Constantly under pressure from the services, the contractors, and the politicians, the office of the Secretary of Defense sometimes puts on pressure of its own to use contractors for political purposes. Perhaps turnabout is fair play, but political pressures have a way of feeding on themselves and thus building up to ever more dangerous levels.

In June 1962, the Kennedy Administration faced a difficult fight on the House floor over the perennial argument about the debt limit. The Administration wanted to raise the limit to $308 billion, and it was being vigorously opposed by most Republicans and many Southern Democrats. Even the Defense Department was enlisted in the fight.

"I returned yesterday afternoon to my office about five o'clock," Republican Representative Ford of Michigan told the House during the debate. "There was a note from my staff indicating that Mr. Wally Edwards, the Chrysler Corporation representative in Washington, wanted me to call him. I returned his call. He said that earlier in the day . . . he had received a call from Mr. Ron Linton, who works for the Defense Department. Mr. Linton allegedly had said to Mr. Edwards, 'Can you find out how the Republicans in the House from Michigan are going to vote on the $308 billion debt limitation proposal?' And he said, 'If they do not vote for the $308 billion, defense contracts in Michigan may be curtailed.' "

Ford said he told Edwards: "The Republicans in Michigan are not going to be blackmailed by this kind of an approach from the Department of Defense." Nor were they. The Michigan Republican delegation opposed the $308 billion debt limit.

In testimony in 1963 before the House Appropriations subcommittee that is charged with overseeing the defense budget, Secretary McNamara stated: "If I may answer the question 'What do I believe to be the proper role of congressional representatives in relation to defense contracting?' I would say this:

"I believe it is quite appropriate for a member of Congress or a group of members of Congress to inquire as to why an award is to be made to one company instead of another company. I don't believe it would be appropriate for the members of Congress to seek to change the award from Company A to Company B contrary to the intent of the law under which we procure, and the law is very clear. We are to procure from the lowest price source, other things being equal, subject to certain special situations such as 'set-asides' for small business, and in certain cases labor surplus areas.

"I think the most important function that a congressional representative or delegation can perform in relation to defense contract awards is not to try to influence the award, because, frankly, we will not be influenced . . . by any representations made to us unless they bear on the extent to which we are complying with the law. If we have failed to examine a fact or have lacked information that can properly be taken into account within the meaning of the law, then we will certainly correct any error in our activity. Beyond that we will not be influenced by anyone's representations to us, whether they be members of Congress or others."

It would indeed be difficult to quarrel with McNamara's statement, but it is an idealized view of a highly charged political situation. If politics does not in fact play a role in defense contracting, every member of Congress has been operating under a severe and costly delusion for many years. What is more, Presidents as well as senators and representatives have injected defense contracts into political campaigns from coast to coast. McNamara himself has participated in the cynical congressional game of taking credit for the awarding of defense contracts. Not only does the aura of politics hang over the defense program; so, too, does a feeling of inevitability. Defense contracts have become in the years since the Korean War a built-in part of the American economy.

"I wish that you could see," Senator Clark of Pennsylvania wrote in 1963 to a friend who is a prominent businessman, "the steady flow of mail which I get, pleading for, or demanding, more defense contracts for Pennsylvania. These letters do not come only from businessmen and contractors. They come from labor unions and working people without jobs who know how much money is being spent on defense, and who have come to think of defense contracts as the only way of bringing new jobs into the state. . . .

"In a sense," Clark continued, "the actions of the military-industrial complex do bring us closer to the danger of war, and make the prospect of peace, and true security in a disarmed world under effective international authority, more remote.

But the complex does not want war; no rational person in this nuclear age does. What the complex wants is defense—and more and more of it. I imagine that they believe that by spending more and more on defense they really are enhancing our security, instead of increasingly endangering it. But intentions are irrelevant with the fate of mankind at stake, and also, ironically, the sound rate of growth of our economy, which in the long run is prejudiced by the diversion of so much of our national income to non-wealth producing activities."

CHAPTER 4

The Defense Department and Industry

NO one knows whether the modern American economy can get along without large defense budgets. It was the spending generated by World War II and not the New Deal pump-priming measures of the 1930's that finally pulled the United States out of the decade-long Great Depression. During the 1940's, in the 1950's and thus far in the 1960's, there has not been a major recession, and all during this period of unprecedented and sustained prosperity military expenditures have been maintained at high levels.

Since the 1930's, the federal budget has been one of the principal forces expanding the American economy. In some years it has been the only "growth industry." Yet it is defense expenditures and not welfare programs that have so greatly enlarged the federal government's role in the economy. When the cost of veterans' benefits, atomic energy programs, and interest payments on the national debt, which is largely a legacy from World War II, are added to current spending on defense, the total amounts to nearly three fourths of the federal budget.

In the 1963 fiscal year, defense spending amounted to $48.3

billion, or 8.5 percent of the $568 billion gross national product that year. Military expenditures as a percentage of the GNP have been quite constant since 1956, ranging from a high of 8.9 percent in 1957 and 1958 to a low of 8.3 percent in 1960. During these years defense spending has generally amounted to about half of the total federal budget.

Although more money was spent on defense in 1963 than at the high point of the Korean War—1953, when military spending totaled $43.6 billion—the cost of the Korean War amounted to from 11 to 12 percent of the gross national product. The largest World War II expenditure of $80 billion in 1945 took a third of the nation's GNP, which then amounted to only $218 billion.

In the 1960's the annual military budgets have been larger than the federal taxes collected each year on all personal incomes. Annual defense spending has amounted to more than nine times the federal expenditures for social security, health, education, welfare, and housing combined and four hundred times the contributions by the United States government to the operations of the United Nations and its specialized agencies and programs. The defense budget amounts to four times the net income earned by all of the farmers in the United States. And a fourth of all federal public works projects are part of the defense program.

The real and personal property held by the military in 1963 had a total value estimated at more than $171 billion. Of that, nearly $135 billion was in equipment and other personal property. Over 30 million acres of land are owned or controlled by the military, and these land holdings are greater than the combined areas of Rhode Island, Delaware, New Jersey, Massachusetts, Vermont, New Hampshire, and Maryland.

In a report published in 1962 the U.S. Arms Control and Disarmament Agency estimated that 7,364,000 men and women, or about 10 percent of the work force, were engaged in employment dealing directly with national defense. Of this total, about

3,000,000 were in the armed forces; 1,171,000 were civilian employees of the Defense Department and the services; and 3,193,000 were employed by defense industries.

The report also noted the major industries in which defense work is concentrated. All of the output of the ordnance industry goes into defense work; 94 percent of the aircraft industry is dependent on defense; 61 percent of the shipping and boating industries; 38 percent of radio communications equipment; 20 percent of scientific instruments; 10 percent of iron and steel; 10 percent of fabricated metals; 10 percent of petroleum; 6 percent of transportation; and 5 percent of all chemical production. In fact, production for defense is a factor of some importance contributing to the economic well-being of practically every major American industry.

In 1960 employment in major defense industries accounted for 30 percent of all manufacturing jobs in Kansas; for 28 percent of the jobs in Washington state; for from 20 to 23 percent in Utah, Arizona, Connecticut, California, and New Mexico; for from 8 to 17 percent of the manufacturing jobs in Oklahoma, Massachusetts, Texas, Missouri, Maryland, Florida, and Colorado.

Within California, which has been getting almost a fourth of all the nation's military contract funds, the concentration of defense employment is even greater. The aircraft industry and other defense work in Southern California account for a third of all the jobs in manufacturing in that part of the state and more than half of the employment in the manufacturing of durable goods alone. And in the San Diego area of Southern California, defense industries account for 70 percent of all manufacturing jobs.

Economists who measured the indirect as well as the direct effect of military spending calculated that it accounts for nearly 59 percent of the employment in the Los Angeles-Long Beach area; 55 percent of the jobs in the entire state of California; and 42 percent in the Seattle area in Washington state where the Boeing Company's headquarters are located and its manufacturing facilities are concentrated.

One hundred companies received nearly three fourths of the $28 billion in military contracts awarded during the 1963 fiscal year. The biggest defense contractor was the Lockheed Aircraft Corporation, which got military orders worth $1.5 billion. Lockheed Aircraft is working on such projects as jet transports and fighters as well as the Polaris missile, the Discoverer satellite, and the Agena space vehicle. In second place was Boeing, with contracts totaling $1.3 billion for work on the Minuteman missile, troop transport planes, and modifications of B-52 bombers. The three other companies with over a billion in contracts each were North American Aviation, General Dynamics, and General Electric. Their work was also on both missile and airplane projects.

In testimony before the Senate Subcommittee on Employment and Manpower in November 1963, Roswell L. Gilpatric, who was then Deputy Secretary of Defense, said that "the greater part of the defense budget is spent for products and services which differ either not at all or not fundamentally from the products used in the civilian economy or for products and services which, although clearly for 'military' end use, employ technologies and skills which have ready applications in nondefense markets." Breaking down the average annual defense spending of about $50 billion in recent years, Gilpatric went on to say that $20 billion is used to pay servicemen and civilian employees; $10 billion for the purchase of such common, mass-produced items as food, clothing, and medicines; and $20 billion for "uniquely military hard goods."

"Even in this category," Gilpatric argued, "a large share, perhaps half or more, goes for products whose manufacturers could, provided the economy was firm, readily convert to civilian markets, as was so successfully done following World War II and the Korean War. I refer here not only to producers of items with commercial counterparts, such as trucks and transport planes, but even to producers of many components of missile, nuclear, and other weapons system."

Murray L. Weidenbaum, senior economist at the Stanford Research Institute and a former Boeing economist, does not take such a sanguine view of the relationship of the defense industries to the rest of the nation's economy. In testimony before the same subcommittee, Weidenbaum estimated that four fifths of the equipment used in World War I "consisted of standard peacetime goods produced in ordinary peacetime production facilities." By World War II, Weidenbaum continued, only half of the needed equipment was off-the-shelf goods. Still, he added, the bulk of military equipment produced for World War II consisted of materials manufactured in ordinary peacetime facilities temporarily converted to wartime production.

"Currently," Weidenbaum concluded, "about 90 percent of the material needs of defense consists of specialized equipment which is produced in special facilities built for the purpose. Moreover, the companies involved were set up for, and their experience is limited to, the design and production of military weapon systems and related aerospace vehicles. As a consequence of the technical requirements of military work, these companies have tremendous numbers of scientists and engineers, compared with the commercial-oriented industries. The typical defense company hires four or five times the number of scientists and engineers as the most technically oriented commercial company to support the same volume of sales."

Weidenbaum also pointed out that efforts by some defense-oriented firms to diversify their operations have failed because the nature of production for the military is so different from the mass production and low-cost characteristics of goods developed for civilian markets.

"For example," Weidenbaum said in his testimony, "the lack of commercial marketing capability of these firms results from their preoccupation with meeting the rigorous technical requirements of the military customer. Their inability to produce large volumes at low cost also reflects their unique capability to design small numbers of large-scale systems of great technical complexity. . . . A new model of refrigerator at half the price of current types may have a large market even if it suffers from significant reductions in quality. The second best missile, in contrast, may hardly be a bargain."

While defense spending has remained at a high but stable level in the period since the Korean War, federal expenditures for research and development (more than half of which is appropriated for military purposes) have increased at a spectacular rate. By 1963 the federal government was supporting 70 percent of all research and development costs in the United States.

In the 1964 fiscal year federal research and development projects totaled $14.9 billion, and half of these funds went to the Defense Department. As recently as 1953 research and development expenditures by the federal government amounted to only $2 billion. During the decade beginning in 1953 these expenditures increased at the rate of a billion a year, with no protest from the generally economy-minded Congress or from businessmen and other taxpayers who usually tell the whole world how weary they are of the revenue burdens they are forced to carry.

"If," John H. Rubel, an Assistant Secretary of Defense, said in 1963, "the federal government were to propose to produce 10 percent of the automobiles, or to make 10 percent of the clothing, or to raise and distribute 10 percent of the food consumed in the United States, I would expect to hear some public discussion. In fact, of course, any such proposal is unthinkable and even the suggestion seems beside the point. It is completely foreign to our conception of the way in which our national economy and our national life should be conducted."

Yet, Rubel went on to note, there has been no protest against the dominant role the federal government—and particularly the Defense Department—has assumed in science in the United States through the rapid increase in expenditures for research and development. The absence of any meaningful discussion of this trend is particularly surprising when it is remembered that Americans have traditionally prided themselves as being a nation of independent-minded inventors and tinkerers. The picture of Thomas Edison stolidly working in his laboratory or of Henry Ford busily engaged in his cluttered garage are part of an American tradition that has been abruptly pushed aside in the race to build bigger and more accurate missiles and to beat the Russians to the moon.

In trying to account for the ease with which Americans have accepted the growing federal role in research and development, Rubel noted that "part of the explanation stems from the readiness of the public and the Congress generally to accept expenditures for national defense with comparatively little debate, convinced that they are probably essential to national survival, that it is 'better to be safe than sorry.' "

He also noted the feeling that research and development expenditures for defense and space will result in widespread "fallout" and "spillover" benefiting the civilian economy as well as the government.

"And, perhaps most important of all," Rubel concluded, "is the fact that about 66 percent of the funds spent for federally-supported research and development are expended by industry. In this sense, the principles of private enterprise are not violated by these federal undertakings. Research and engineering, which are regarded as business expenses in the private sector, now represent enormous business opportunities to firms furnishing research and development services and material to the government."

Not only do federal research and development contracts represent big, new business for American industry, they also have become important sources of revenue and prestige for colleges and universities. There is hardly an institution of higher learning in the country, no matter how small or specialized it may be, that has not received a federal contract. Fifteen percent of all federal research and development money goes to colleges and universities.

The high level of defense spending since the Korean War has not, however, meant that production and employment have been stable throughout the industries that have been so dependent on military appropriations. During the 1950's the emphasis on military spending shifted from such mass-produced hardware as tanks, trucks, and airplanes to highly sophisticated missile systems. This meant that the automobile industry and the other producers of durable goods, with their heavy concentration in the Midwest, lost defense dollars to the West Coast where airplane manufacturers were able to convert with relative ease to the development and production of missiles and where the electronics industries so important to missiles were already concentrated. The New England states also benefited from the new emphasis on missiles—particularly from the boom in electronics to provide guidance systems for the missiles.

On a percentage basis, however, the Mountain states gained the most. Defense Department figures show that in the 1962 fiscal year the Mountain states got 90 percent more in military-contract funds than they had received in the 1958 fiscal year. The next largest increase was in New England, where the percentage of defense money went up more than 50 percent during the same five-year period. Defense business in the South Atlantic states increased by one third, while in the Pacific Coast states the increase was almost one fourth. Meanwhile, the smaller Midwestern states suffered a sharp decline in defense business and even the larger, more industrialized states of the Midwest failed to keep up with the relatively modest increase in defense business on the West Coast, where military hardware as well as research has been a major reason for that area's rapid expansion during the last twenty-five years.

The shift in the regional patterns of defense spending during the 1950's was not without its economic and political repercussions. The troubles of the automobile industry in the middle and late 1950's, particularly the difficulties besetting the Chrysler Corporation, were caused in part by the loss of defense business.

Not only are the governors and congressmen from the Midwest seeking defense work, they also are attempting to stimulate research activities in the Midwest because, as businessmen on both the East and West Coasts have discovered, defense contracts frequently follow research awards in today's highly sophisticated world of weapons.

State congressional delegations also keep up the pressure on the Pentagon to introduce regional balances in the awarding of defense contracts. The New York congressional delegation, for example, frequently writes Secretary McNamara to point out that New York's share of military contracts slipped slightly in a month, or perhaps remained the same, while the share of defense business going to California increased.

For more than a century open competition for government contracts has been recognized as the best method to assure honest and efficient spending of public funds—although some defense agencies, notably the Navy, have long preferred other methods. But as the defense program expanded and as the sophistication of weapons increased, competitive bidding steadily decreased. The Pentagon favors negotiating contracts with suppliers it decides are best qualified to do the work.

The Pentagon preference for negotiated contracts began in 1948 after Congress passed a bill which, as President Truman noted at the time, granted "unprecedented freedom from specific procurement restrictions during peacetime."

"That freedom," Truman pointed out in letters to the Secretaries of the Army, Navy, and Air Force, "is given to permit the flexibility and latitude needed in present-day national defense activities. The basic need, however, remains to assure favorable price and adequate service to the government. To the degree that restrictions have been diminished, therefore, responsibility upon the defense establishment has been increased. There is danger that the natural desire for flexibility and speed in procurement will lead to excessive placement of contracts by negotiation and undue reliance upon large concerns, and this must not occur. For these reasons, I am asking you to specify detailed standards to guide your procurement officers concerning the placing of business with small concerns and the circumstances under which they may waive the general policy of advertising for bids."

Despite Truman's warning, negotiated contracts have become the modern way of military procurement. In the last ten years the services have spent nearly all (the annual figures range from 84 to 89 percent) of their funds for defense goods and services obtained through negotiated contracts. Many of the contracts do result from design and cost competitions, but these are limited and the results are not binding on the officials making the procurement decisions.

In the 1963 fiscal year, for example, negotiated contracts accounted for 87 percent of the value of all the contracts awarded by the Defense Department. Five companies received contracts amounting to almost a fourth of the value of all the awards and nearly three fourths of the contract funds went to one hundred companies.

There are many valid reasons for the letting of contracts through negotiation rather than after publicly advertised competitive bidding. Many modern weapons cannot be bought off a shelf, as Congress recognized in 1948 when it granted the military the widespread authority it now has to negotiate contracts. But this authority, which the services had assured

Congress would be used sparingly, has become the preferred Pentagon method for letting contracts.

Often, a contractor is chosen to develop a weapon and then allowed to produce it without any Pentagon effort to find out whether he can do the job better and cheaper than anyone else. Sometimes in such situations close relationships develop between the contractor and the military service he is working for, and military officers and civilian employees of the services cross over to take better-paying jobs with industry.

Competitive bidding not only avoids compromising involvements, it almost always saves the taxpayers money. After studying a series of cases where competitive buying replaced negotiated contracts, the General Accounting Office concluded that competition means average savings to the government of 25 percent.

Some of the savings that have resulted from competition were even greater. The price of fluid for hydraulic equipment on airplanes dropped from $25 to $15 a gallon when competitive bids were sought before purchases were made. Electric motors went down from $614 to $280, a reduction of 54 percent. Eight-inch howitzers declined in price from $68,044 to $41,415, or by 39 percent. Fins for the Talos missile cost $1,360 when purchased competitively. This was a drop of 32 percent from the negotiated figure of $1,998.99, which obviously was not the bargain-basement price that it would seem to be at first glance.

One of the most outspoken and persistent advocates of competitive bidding was former Republican Representative Earl Wilson of Indiana. A rotund man in his fifties and a flamboyant speaker, Wilson became interested in Defense Department procurement habits when a friend of his lost out on a contract year after year through dealings that eventually were proved to be illegal.

Among the cases that have since been cited by Wilson was one involving the Collins Radio Company of Cedar Rapids, Iowa. The Navy negotiated a contract with Collins for the development of an advanced and highly sensitive walkie-talkie radio. When the radio was successfully developed at a cost of a million dollars, the Navy decided not to seek competitive bids for the construction of 670 sets that it wanted built immediately. Instead, the Navy negotiated another contract with Collins. Wilson contended that the Navy's failure to seek competitive bids cost the taxpayers an additional and unnecessary million dollars.

"I had a Navy rear admiral tell me," Wilson said in a House speech in 1963, ". . . that he is consistently amazed at the way Collins anticipates and is able to get sole-source contracts to fill present and future requirements of the Navy. In the next breath he admitted that Collins seldom, if ever, wins a competitive procurement, and he admitted that at least 134 Collins employees are former Navy employees. . . . In short, the inference here is plain, here is a company with a locked-up inside track to Navy money."

At Wilson's request, the GAO counted the former Navy officers and civilian employees who went to work for Collins in the six-year period from 1957 to 1962. Included among the 134 former Navy men the GAO found on the Collins payroll were a rear admiral, a captain, a design engineer, and several former commanders, contract negotiators, radio engineers, and other technicians skilled in the Navy's ways.

In discussing the Collins case Wilson emphasized that, so far as he could tell, no laws were violated and all of the dealings were carried out according to well-established rules. But, he added, "one of those rules is evidently to hire ex-service people who have friends and influence inside procurement sections."

The movement of officers and civilian employees from the Pentagon to the defense industries is a costly drain on the government. Every important defense contractor has retired generals or admirals, colonels or commanders on his payroll. Civilian specialists who have learned their way through the

73

labyrinth of Pentagon procedures also forsake government service for the better-paying defense industries. The Defense Department has no control over what civilians can do when they leave government employment, and regulations applying to the activities of retired officers prohibit them only from participating in direct buying and selling activities involving the services.

The most recent count of retired officers employed by companies doing business with the Pentagon was made by a House Armed Services subcommittee. In a 1960 report it listed 1,426 retired officers on the payrolls of the hundred largest military contractors. General Dynamics alone employed 186 retired officers, including three generals and twenty admirals. Lockheed had 171 retired officers, five of them generals and twenty-two admirals. North American Aviation had eighty-four retired officers on its payroll; two of them were generals, six were admirals. Boeing's list of retired officers totaled seventy-two and included two generals and three admirals. Salaries were uniformly good, too. They ranged up to $100,000 a year.

In commenting on testimony taken both from retired officers who went to work for defense contractors and from officials of the companies, the Armed Services subcommittee, headed by Democratic Representative F. Edward Hébert of Louisiana, noted in its report:

"We were impressed with several obvious inconsistencies in testimony. Some might have a more felicitous term.

"For example, when discussing influence: some retired officers contended that the retired officer is a 'has-been'; that he has no influence; and that his personal contact is resented by the active-duty personnel. These witnesses contended that the fact of being retired was, in itself, a handicap, if not a deterrent.

"But these confident conclusions were watered down by most of these witnesses, who, while testifying that they knew of no instances of attempted influence on themselves while on active duty, nevertheless agreed that a 'cooling-off' period was desirable.

"It is a little difficult to reconcile these assurances about 'has-beens,' when it is agreed that they could stand to be 'cooled off' for, say, two years.

"How does one rationalize a 'has-been' with current 'technical competence' in the vast, complex, and fast-developing field of military requirements if the 'has-been' is, in fact, shut off from current military thinking?

"These retired officers are either 'has-beens' or 'up-to-date.' They cannot be both. The 'has-been' would deal in old concepts; but the 'up-to-date' retiree would be current. There is only one source of current information: active military officials. Surely industry is not employing historians at lush salaries. Industry buys what the employee knows. It buys knowledge which can be converted into sales for a profit. . . .

"We entertained no thought that any retired officer or retired civilian official would publicly confess being influenced while in office; or, indeed, that while preoccupied with making his decisions, he would recognize the presence of influence. The better grade and more expensive influence is a very subtle thing when successfully applied. It often happens that position, place, and even entertainment have a role.

"The 'coincidence' of contracts and personal contacts with firms represented by retired officers and retired civilian officials sometimes raises serious doubts as to the complete objectivity of some of these decisions."

The report stated further that the members of the subcommittee "think it unethical and unconscionable for a person to have anything to do in private life with a subject with which he was directly concerned while in public employment" and urged Congress to enact stringent regulations involving the post-retirement employment of Pentagon civilian employees as well as officers. But the proposed changes in existing regulations were never approved by Congress.

The influence of so-called "advisory" councils to the Defense Department and to the services presents problems not much different from those involved in the hiring of retired officers by industry. Senator Williams of Delaware once called attention to the unbelievable size of surplus feather stocks owned by the military and suggested that one reason for the surplus might have been an advisory board on wartime feather needs, which turned out to be made up of feather merchants who appeared to be feathering their own nests.

Although advisory committees always raise difficult questions about possible conflicts of interest, McNamara established a major new one at the Pentagon in 1962. It is the Defense Advisory Council, and among its twenty members are officials of companies with big defense contracts.

The twenty-member council includes officials of such large defense contractors as the Westinghouse Electric Corporation, Aerojet-General Corporation, Chrysler Corporation, and Olin Mathieson Chemical Corporation. Defense Department officials have insisted that the council serves largely as a forum for the presentation of general Pentagon procurement problems and for the discussion of suggestions and criticisms of procurement practices from companies and industries deeply involved in defense contracting. Former Deputy Defense Secretary Gilpatric has acknowledged, however, that the council's establishment raised "certain legal and ethical considerations" but declared that its operations had been "most circumspect."

Although little public information is made available about the council's operations, its meetings apparently have been devoted to the discussion of legitimate problems involving defense contracts and have not resulted in any instances of undue industry influence. But the danger is ever present when the relations between defense contractors and the Pentagon are so close and so constant.

The loose contracting and subcontracting practices that mushroomed in the 1950's along with the missile race also led to pyramiding of profits in some instances. Contractors were allowed not only to take their usual profits on work they did themselves; they also were permitted to take the same profit margin on work done for them by subcontractors who of course had added their own profit onto the prices they charged the contractors.

With the development of complicated missiles, it quickly became clear that none of the armed services had the technical capacity to build such sophisticated weapons, or even to direct in any detail the scientific and production activities necessary for modern missile weaponry. So all of the services contracted out most of this costly work, following a system the Air Force had used successfully during and immediately after World War II. An integral part of the new approach to weaponry was the "systems" concept. Under this concept the management and development of a new weapons system was carried out under the direction of a company selected by the Army, Navy, or Air Force. The company also was responsible for obtaining all the parts for the weapons system, generally through subcontracts.

In 1963 Admiral Rickover told the House Defense Appropriations subcommittee about the pyramiding of profits within the divisions of a company with which the Navy had negotiated a contract. Most of the work was to be done by one of the divisions of the corporation. (Rickover did not identify the company.) The division responsible for carrying out the contract quoted a price to the Navy, said it included 15 percent profit, and noted that some of the work would be done by other divisions of the company.

"Each one of these other divisions submitted its costs, plus its profit, to the lead or selling division," Rickover testified. "We found that no attempt was being made to get prices from outside sources for these parts and no real check was being made of the reasonableness of the estimated cost by the various other divisions. In fact, prices from other divisions, including profits, were taken at face value by the lead division and we were being asked to pay profit on the other division's profits."

A detailed study of the pyramiding of profits in the production of missiles was made in 1962 by the Senate Investigations subcommittee headed by Democratic Senator John L. McClellan of Arkansas. The subcommittee carefully examined the Army's contracting and subcontracting procedures for the production of Nike missiles, antiaircraft weapons in the years immediately following World War II but now being developed into antimissile weapons. They have still not been perfected as antimissile defenses, however.

Western Electric Company, a subsidiary of American Telephone & Telegraph Company that makes equipment for the Bell System, has been the prime contractor for the Nike program. From 1950 to 1962 the Army paid out a total of more than $1.5 billion to Western Electric for work on the Nike system. But Western Electric did only the electronics work for the system, amounting to about one fourth of the entire Nike cost over the twelve-year period.

The electronics package was one of four major subsystems making up the Nike weapon program. The other subsystems constituted the aeronautical, mechanical, and automotive parts. These parts of the Nike program were subcontracted by Western Electric largely to Douglas Aircraft Company, which produced the aeronautical subsystem but in turn subcontracted the automotive system to the Fruehauf Corporation, and the mechanical system to Consolidated Western Steel, a division of the United States Steel Corporation. The producers of the three subcontracted subsystems delivered them directly to the Army.

Western Electric's profit on the Nike contracts over the twelve years totaled $112 million, a not unreasonable 7.9 percent of the entire $1.5 billion contract. But the $112 million amounted to 31 percent of the $359 million worth of electrical equipment actually produced by Western Electric, which, according to customary business practices, also took a profit on all of the items produced by the subcontractors.

Douglas received orders from Western Electric totaling $645 million for the production of the aeronautical, mechanical, and automotive subsystems. Eighty-three percent of these funds, however, were used to pay the costs of contracts that Douglas in turn farmed out to sub-subcontractors. So, although the Douglas profit figure of 7.6 percent on the entire $645 million worth of contracts seemed perfectly reasonable, its total profit of $46 million actually amounted to 44 percent of the $103 million in contracts that it fulfilled itself. But the profit-pyramiding in the Nike program did not end even here.

"By this contracting device, at least three separate profits were paid on the Nike trailers," the Senate Investigations subcommittee report noted. "The automotive subsystems were produced by Fruehauf Corporation as a sub-subcontract under Douglas and Western Electric. It cost Fruehauf $49.3 million to produce many thousands of Nike trailers between 1950 and 1960. Fruehauf was allowed a profit of $4.5 million. These costs were invoiced to Douglas who performed no work on the trailers but added a pyramided profit of $3.7 million because the Fruehauf invoices became a part of the Douglas cost base upon which profits are computed. Douglas in turn forwarded its invoices for its 'costs' (including Fruehauf's) to Western Electric Company, the prime contractor. Western's cost base was increased by these Douglas-Fruehauf subcontracts and it took a third profit on the trailers amounting to $3.3 million. The $49.3 million in trailers produced by Fruehauf thus bore three separate profit loads: $4.5 million to the producer; $3.7 million to the nonproducing subcontractor; $3.3 million to the nonproducing prime contractor. The total profits amounted to $11.5 million—in excess of 23 percent over complete costs."

The subcommittee report pointed out that in 1959 the Army

finally sought competitive bids in purchasing some of the trailers that Fruehauf had been producing for the Nike project. (The trailers were fairly standardized units into which complicated electronic gear was then built.) Fruehauf had been charging the Army, through Douglas and Western Electric, from $10,300 to $12,000 for each trailer. When the trailer project was thrown open to competitive bidding, the low bid, submitted by the Henney Motor Company of New York, turned out to be only $5,304, or less than half the average price the Army had been paying Fruehauf.

It, of course, costs money for a contractor to administer and oversee subcontracts. Both the Western Electric and Douglas contracts, however, included provisions for the government to pay for such administrative costs before profits were to be figured.

Officials of both Western Electric and Douglas defended their taking of profits on subcontracts by noting that this is the customary way to figure profits. They also said in testimony before the Senate subcommittee that neither the Defense Department nor the Renegotiation Board, the federal agency that reviews defense contracts and profits, found anything wrong with the arrangements criticized by the Senate investigators as the pyramiding of profits. But the Western Electric and Douglas arguments did not convince Senator McClellan, the subcommittee chairman, and he demanded further explanations, particularly from Douglas.

In answering McClellan's criticism of the company's profits on missile production, Donald Douglas, Jr., the president of Douglas Aircraft, included advertising as a necessary expense that should be paid by the government. Douglas went on to maintain that the government ought to finance even more of a defense contractor's advertising expenses than is now allowed. For the most part, advertising can be charged off to a defense contract only if it is limited to the recruiting of scientists and engineers and other workers.

"However," wrote Douglas in his reply to McClellan's criticisms of his company's profits, "our advertising is more properly labeled as institutional in character. Certainly, it is obvious that we cannot expect an observer of one of our advertisements in a magazine or newspaper to rush to the nearest dealer and buy a commercial airplane, a military aircraft, a missile, or a space vehicle. Then, why do we advertise, and why do companies engaged entirely in government work also advertise? All of us would prefer not to spend these dollars which are not allowed in pricing our government work, but we have found it necessary to do so. . . .

"One of the principal methods for acquainting the public at large with the important role our company plays in our economy and in our national defense is through our advertising," Douglas argued. "Experience has shown that this enables us to attract and retain more qualified employees. In a sense, it can fairly be said that our advertising identified our personnel with the defense of their country in much the same way that his uniform identifies the soldier, sailor, or airman. This identification also adds to the desire of each employee to do a better job—to turn out better products and services on a more timely basis and at lower costs. . . . The relationship to government contracts is also evidenced by the fact that some of our advertising is done in coordination with the military services. It is another way of letting the public know what the military is doing to provide an adequate defense for our country. For all of these reasons, we sincerely believe that our institutional-type advertising should be recognized in the pricing of government work."

In further attempting to justify his company's profits on the Nike contracts, Douglas maintained that the development costs of his firm's civilian aircraft, including even the DC-3, which was placed on the market in the 1930's and has not been changed in any basic way since then, contributed to the company's ability to carry out a missile contract. Therefore, concluded Douglas, part of the cost of developing the DC-3 could properly be charged off to the Nike work. Douglas may have convinced himself, but he did not convince McClellan of the relevance of this sort of an argument.

Said McClellan in a statement commenting on the claims made by Douglas:

"The inability to obtain consistent testimony prompted the chairman to insist that Douglas Aircraft Company prepare and submit to the subcommittee a specific breakdown of these alleged unreimbursed costs so that a proper determination could be made as to whether the $63.8 million Western Electric company claimed it paid to Douglas as profit was in fact reduced by $34.01 million in disallowable costs incurred by Douglas Aircraft in performing the Nike contracts. . . .

"It is noted that over $23 million of the claimed reduction in profit is assigned to costs incurred in developing the DC-8 commercial jet aircraft and another $2 million relates to costs incurred in connection with the DC-7 commercial aircraft, DC-6 commercial aircraft, and even the DC-3 commercial aircraft— the latter of which is a pre-World War II development. . . .

"The attempt of Mr. Douglas to minimize the size of his company's real profits is entirely unsupported by the facts. His attempt to charge expenses of commercial endeavors of his company against his actual profit on the Nike missile production in an effort to diminish or conceal the true nature and extent of his missile profit is improper and unjustified and cannot be approved or allowed to stand.

"The system of procurement which would permit the taking of profits in that fashion surely requires prompt revision and correction."

Yet, the Douglas and Western Electric profits were allowed to stand. The taking of profits by prime contractors on work done by subcontractors has become an accepted part of the defense program. Most taxpayers, those who after all pay these profits, undoubtedly would agree with Senator McClellan that such profit-taking is difficult to defend.

But even the McClellan subcommittee failed to come up with any answer to the problem of profit pyramiding. The subcommittee only suggested that the President appoint "a high-level study group to reassess the government's procurement practices."

"The advanced technology of the space age, requiring huge expenditures of federal funds," the subcommittee observed in its report, "has created between government and contractors new relationships to accomplish research and development and carry out production. The contract has, in effect, become a quasi-governmental service agency, usually operating without competition in supplying major weapons systems. The rule of the marketplace quite evidently no longer applies to the procurement of modern weapons. The contracts which provide them can no longer be considered commercial transactions between buyer and seller and there is now need for spelling out a new legal, economic relationship."

All of this does not necessarily mean that defense contractors in general have been making excessive profits. In fact, nobody seems to know for sure whether the overall profit figures are too large or too small, but the Defense Department has been conducting studies to try to determine actual profit rates on military contracts.

Some available figures have indicated that the typical profit on defense business is rather modest. For example, 4,680 contractors who did a total defense business amounting to more than $32 billion for the fiscal year 1963 have had their contracts audited or renegotiated. Their combined profits came to $917 million, or 2.9 percent—and this was before taxes and before the deduction of any costs that might be disallowed by the government. Moreover, almost $7 billion worth of business resulted in losses for the contractors, a loss amounting to 6.6 percent of the money paid them by the government, before taxes and before their contracts had been reviewed by the Renegotiation Board.

Before anyone can decide, however, whether a profit of less than 3 percent on sales is too much or too little, a lot of other questions have to be examined—such as the return on invested capital and the value of special assistance provided by the government to certain contractors. Frequently, for instance, the Defense Department furnishes equipment or facilities, or helps in the financing of defense work by making advance payments to contractors. As Admiral Rickover has pointed out, profits may be hidden in cost figures that often are all but impossible for the government to check.

"Extensive profits can be hidden in costs just by the way overhead is charged or how component parts or material are priced," Rickover told the House Defense Appropriations subcommittee in 1963. "The government agency may never know how much profit the contractor makes in producing it."

Rickover has been especially critical of the way the cost of constructing buildings and other defense facilities for the government so often turns out to be much higher than the original estimates. These contracts are generally awarded after bids are obtained through advertisements, but all of the contracts provide for price increases if there are changes in design or if unusual problems are encountered once a project is under way.

Rickover maintained that "a good deal of the construction contracting today is bid on the basis that the contractor expects he will get additional large sums of money on every contract through changes and claims. He not only expects to exploit unnecessary changes due to the work, the weather, and job conditions, but will devote considerable effort searching for unreasonable interpretations of the plans and the specifications and other imaginary 'changes.' "

Defense costs are also often increased by building into equipment marginal or unnecessary features. Sometimes such "gold-plating" can be defended in terms of safety or performance, but frequently—as the result of inefficiency or laziness in the Pentagon—an item that could be produced on the assembly line remains a custom-made job because that is what it was when limited production began.

Some instances of safe and economical cost-cutting can be cited: A commercial hydraulic device replaced the specially designed electronic "mule" for opening and closing the underground Minuteman missile silos, and the cost of each "mule" dropped from $555,000 to $80,800. A similar substitution cut the cost of a lift truck for another missile from $2,480 to $385. When excess capacity in a brake-fluid container for the T-38 airplane was eliminated, costs per unit were reduced from $175 to $52.

Defense spending extends into so much of the American economy that it is difficult to find critics of military waste either in the Congress or within the executive branch of the government itself. The few critics of wasteful defense practices who raised their voices during the 1950's were quickly reminded that a too hasty demobilization accompanied by a penny-pinching approach to the armed forces when World War II ended seriously jeopardized the early United States effort in the Korean War.

So, fueled by the bitter memories of the Korean War experience and propelled by the exploding technology of jets and missiles, the United States embarked during the 1950's on the largest peacetime defense program in the history of any nation. Not until the early 1960's were questions raised about the ultimate direction and end of the program, and these questions came from quite an unexpected source.

CHAPTER 5

McNamara: the Man in the Middle

WHEN Robert S. McNamara became Secretary of Defense in 1961, he stepped into what he later described as "a jungle." The rivalries among the services were intense. Civilian control over their activities had been minimal for a decade or more. If a general or an admiral could not bend the wills of the civilian officials in the Pentagon, he ran to Capitol Hill where he could generally be sure of a sympathetic hearing. Congress sometimes gave the Defense Department even more money than the enormous sums it requested year after year. The additional funds were to be used for pet projects being advanced by one or the other of the services.

The military-industrial complex that so concerned President Eisenhower when he left the White House in 1961 had its greatest growth during his eight years as President. Now, in the 1960's, Americans have become accustomed to defense spending of $50 billion or more a year.

But it was not only the Korean War and the missile race that sent defense spending soaring. None of the three men who served as Secretary of Defense under Eisenhower was ever able to assert his civilian authority over the military. The late

Charles E. Wilson came the closest to doing so, but even bull-headed old "Engine Charlie" was never quite on top of the Pentagon military bureaucracy. Throughout the 1950's the Army, Navy, and Air Force were able to generate support on Capitol Hill by using the pressure of firms with which the services had contracts. Frequently these pressures from defense contractors increased spending above the ceilings set by the Secretary of Defense.

Neil H. McElroy, the Proctor & Gamble Company executive who succeeded Wilson, was particularly weak. The conflicting pressures on him from the Army and the Air Force were so great that he finally threw up his hands and asked Congress to make up his mind for him and decide which of the two services' competing and almost identical missiles, Jupiter or Thor, should be put into production. The record of Thomas S. Gates, Jr., the Wall Street investment banker who succeeded McElroy, was little better.

Washington was not particularly surprised or shocked by the failures of Eisenhower's succession of Secretaries of Defense. In the immediate postwar years the job, which was then not nearly so immense as it has since become, drove the first Secretary of Defense, James V. Forrestal, to his death. He was succeeded by Louis A. Johnson, a politician-lawyer from West Virginia who distinguished himself by dismantling the nation's defenses on what turned out to be the eve of the Korean War. General George C. Marshall and New York lawyer Robert A. Lovett, the other two Secretaries of Defense during the Truman Administration, spent all of their time dealing with the Korean War.

On Capitol Hill the Senate and House Armed Services Committees are supposed to oversee the Defense Department, but all except a few members of the two committees are themselves part of the military-industrial complex. Men with a special interest in military matters vie for positions on the committees.

In 1964 a total of 112 members of Congress, almost a fourth

of the Senate and the House, held reserve commissions. Thirty-five of them were in the Marine Corps, thirty-four in the Army, twenty-three in the Air Force, and twenty in the Navy. President Johnson himself has held a reserve commission as a Navy commander ever since he served briefly in the Navy during World War II. The congressional reservists wore two hats, military and civilian, and many of them became active lobbyists on Capitol Hill for their services. But it was not until November 1964 that McNamara finally decided that members of Congress should not hold reserve commissions because it is unlikely that they would be called to active service in time of war.

The military services themselves often press for committee appointments for senators and representatives they consider particularly friendly to them. Once on the Armed Services Committees, assignments eagerly sought by new members every two years, the senators and representatives know that their states and districts are more likely to get defense contracts if they behave themselves as committee members. This means giving the military what it wants.

So unusual is it for members of the Armed Services Committees to challenge the ruling hierarchy of the committees that when four representatives did question the House Armed Services Committee majority in 1964, they soon became known as the "fearless four." These were four Democratic members of the committee who opposed the decision to increase from $5 to $52 million the authorization of Air Force expenditures to develop a new bomber. The four representatives, who also tried to reduce other defense authorizations on a selective basis, were Samuel S. Stratton and Otis G. Pike, both of New York; Jeffrey Cohelan of California, and Lucien N. Nedzi of Michigan. In a similar, and similarly unsuccessful, fight on the House floor in 1963 they were joined by Democratic Representative Richard H. Ichord of Missouri, who in 1964 decided that more money was needed to develop a new bomber.

"The Armed Services Committees are a patsy for the Pentagon," Republican Representative Thomas B. Curtis of Missouri has said. "Every member needs an up-check from the Pentagon. This is a locked-in deal."

In less colorful English, this means that the Pentagon treats members of the Armed Services Committees like kings. Senator Russell has been hauled around at taxpayers' expense in luxurious Air Force planes so that he could fill speaking engagements with a minimum of effort. Committee members frequently are invited, along with other senators and representatives, to spend weekends touring military installations.

"When the Air Force gets into some sort of trouble," Democratic Representative Henry Reuss of Wisconsin once said, "they always want you to come out and visit their war room in Omaha."

One senator, who resisted Air Force blandishments for several years but finally decided to go along on a weekend tour with eight other senators just to see how his tax dollars were being spent, found a chauffeured Air Force car waiting for him at his home on the Friday morning the junket began. A colonel was assigned to look after the comforts of each senator.

Breakfast, complete with a linen table cloth, was served on the jet on the way to Florida. Drinks were available for the senators and colonels who might need eye-openers. Throughout the tour, Air Force photographers were on hand, ready to take pictures of senators with generals and weapons. From Florida to Nebraska to Colorado to California, there were cocktail parties, steak dinners, brandy, and cigars.

The Senate and House Defense Appropriations subcommittees, which provide the money for the military after the Armed Services Committees have authorized the expenditure of the funds, are just as sympathetic toward the military as are the Armed Services Committees. There is also considerable overlapping in the membership. Senator Russell is chairman of both the Senate Armed Services Committee and the Senate

Defense Appropriations subcommittee. There is little room for checks and balances in such a situation.

Neither the Armed Services Committees nor the Defense Appropriations subcommittees have more than a handful of staff assistants. Adequate preparations are seldom made for the appropriations hearings by either the staffs or the members of the subcommittees. Consequently, the sessions are frequently taken up with such momentous questions as the one raised by Democratic Senator Allen J. Ellender of Louisiana at a Senate hearing in 1963.

"To what extent, if any, are helicopters taking the place of automobiles in transferring generals and colonels from one spot to another?" he asked Assistant Secretary of Defense Charles J. Hitch. "I play golf at the Army-Navy Club, and every five minutes during the weekend there is one passing over."

In the fall of 1964 the Air Force tried to mend a few fences and make some more friends among the members of the staffs of congressional committees by taking ten staff members on a nineteen-day, all expenses paid tour of Air Force bases in the Pacific. The committees represented on the trip included Senate and House groups dealing with such diverse subjects as small business, investigations, and military operations as well as constitutional rights and the operations of the Post Office.

The Armed Services Committees have almost always sided with the generals and the admirals in their many disputes over the years with the civilian leadership in the Pentagon. So it was not surprising that the Senate Armed Services Committee was the center of a knot of opposition on Capitol Hill to the ratification of the test-ban treaty in 1963. Within the Kennedy Administration, Air Force generals were the principal opponents of the treaty, and the generals were given a forum by the Preparedness subcommittee of the Senate Armed Services Committee. The subcommittee chairman is Democratic Senator John Stennis of Mississippi, a ranking member of the parent

Armed Services Committee, and he held hearings concurrently with the principal hearings on the treaty conducted by the Senate Foreign Relations Committee.

The Preparedness subcommittee's hearings were far more than just a Capitol Hill sideshow. The power of its parent Armed Services Committee is so feared it was thought for a time that the hearings of its subcommittee would lead to widespread opposition to the treaty. But, as it turned out, Senator Russell and Senator Stennis were the only important Senate leaders to vote against the treaty. The Armed Services Committee's efforts to build a backlash to the treaty were still significant, however, because they dramatically showed the power of the military—and particularly the Air Force—to get the kind of hearings it wanted and to use them as the generals saw fit.

In addition to engaging in such maneuvering as its efforts to defeat the test-ban treaty, the Air Force has been trying to move in on the civilian space program. Lobbying by the Air Force and its contractors helped to prolong the life of the Dyna-Soar manned space flight program for a year. Boeing was the prime contractor for Dyna-Soar, a project that largely duplicated the Space Agency's Gemini program.

Appearing before the House Defense Appropriations subcommittee in 1963, Secretary McNamara expressed doubt about continuing Dyna-Soar (it was canceled later that year) "when we have another program that will provide for the accomplishment of most of what the first will do." But phalanxes of Air Force officers had already done their lobbying in the offices of influential senators and representatives not only for Dyna-Soar but for Air Force participation in the Space Agency's Gemini program.

Representative Thomas of Texas, who knows something about lobbying himself, objected to the Air Force intrusion. When McNamara protested that Air Force participation would be limited "to operations in the near-earth orbit," Thomas was incensed.

"Do you mean to say that when the camel gets its nose under the tent, it is going to stop there and not go any farther?" the Congressman asked. "Mr. Secretary, you know human nature and the Air Force do not work like that. My understanding is that the colonels and lieutenant colonels were walking in the halls of the House and Senate talking up this project. . . . The very idea of the biggest spending agency in government sending representatives here telling the Congress what to do!"

As chairman of the House Appropriations subcommittee that handles the National Aeronautics and Space Administration budget, Thomas has more than a casual interest in an expanding civilian space program. To reward him for his efforts on its behalf, NASA, it will be remembered, located its Manned Spacecraft Center in his congressional district.

Backing up the armed services in their insistent demands for more of everything are not only the individual defense contractors and their workers, the latter often represented by such powerful unions as the United Automobile Workers and the International Association of Machinists, but also nongovernmental service organizations set up to protect and advance military interests.

The Air Force Association, made up of Air Force officers, retired officers, and Air Force contractors and financed largely by the contractors, provides a clearing house for the interests of the Air Force and the men who do business with it. Each year the AFA holds a convention in Washington which is addressed by the top Air Force officers. The 1963 session in the Sheraton-Park Hotel, where the lobbies were crowded with elaborate displays put up by corporations holding contracts for Air Force weapons and projects, turned into a rallying point for opposition to the test-ban treaty being debated by the Senate at the time of the convention.

The AFA passed a resolution denouncing the treaty as "adherence to a policy of nuclear stalemate" and constituting "an open invitation to Soviet aggression on terms which the free world cannot meet and is not prepared to meet." The resolution went on to say that "a stalemate strategy is illusory on both political and technological grounds" and that "strong measures must be taken to insure that our strategic superiority, in the meaningful area of nuclear striking forces, is preserved." Not surprisingly, the AFA also deplored the fact that "manned offensive strategic systems are likely to be phased out completely."

"Holding these beliefs," the AFA resolution concluded, "we of the Air Force Association are particularly troubled both by the substance of the proposed test-ban treaty and the manner in which it has been thrust upon the Congress, our military leadership, and upon the American people. Much of the basic information pertinent to a prudent decision remains in contention. We are keenly aware of the military risks which are inherent in this treaty. The political gains which are supposed to outweigh these risks are not so clear. Whenever a nation limits its freedom of technical initiative in any important field, its security is endangered. It is our conviction, therefore, that even if the promised safeguards should materialize, ratification of the proposed test-ban treaty would entail unacceptable risks to the security of this nation and of the free world."

So harsh and ill-tempered was the AFA's denunciation of the test-ban treaty that Secretary of the Air Force Eugene M. Zuckert abruptly canceled plans to attend a reception held by the association the next day. "Because I know the association is capable of better things," Zuckert wrote to the AFA, "its resort in this case to irrationalism, which can only lead to passionate rather than reasoned discussion, leaves me no alternative but to cancel my scheduled participation in the Air Force Association program."

But it was not the first time that the AFA and the Air Force, whose views the association reflects, violently and publicly disagreed with the civilians who are supposed to be in ultimate control of military policy. In 1960, for example, the AFA listed its demands: "SAC must be modernized, dispersed, and hardened, with a substantial portion made mobile on the ground and in the air. ICBM production and deployment must be accelerated. The B-70 Mach 3 bomber program must ... be given stature as a full-fledged weapon system. The number of aircraft maintained on airborne alert must be raised to a meaningful level—at least double the present programed rate."

With Kennedy's firm support, McNamara had killed Air Force plans to put Minuteman ICBM's on railroad cars so that they could be constantly on the move and thus presumably considerably more difficult for Russians to hit. McNamara also vetoed a production program for B-70's and, again with Kennedy's firm support, ended the costly Skybolt program for a ballistic missile to be launched from an airplane. Just three months after the AFA's denunciation of the test-ban treaty, McNamara canceled the Air Force's pet space project, Dyna-Soar.

At its 1964 meeting, which was also held at Washington's Sheraton-Park Hotel, the Air Force Association was notably subdued. It contented itself with tepid policy statements expressing concern over the lack of "sufficiently high momentum" in the development of military technology. The Association's president, W. Randolph Lovelace II, noted in presenting the 1964 resolutions that the AFA was under "close scrutiny" in an election year and should rise "above political partisanship."

The AFA is not the only group outside the government promoting the Air Force. Another powerful organization on the Air Force side is the Aerospace Industries Association, which includes both space and Air Force contractors.

Shortly after World War II the Air Force set up the Rand Corporation (for research and development), which from its handsome headquarters in Santa Monica, California, still provides academiclike studies buttressing whatever arguments the Air Force wants surrounded with political, economic, or strategic justifications. So successful has Rand been as a prop to the Air Force that the Navy later set up its Center for Naval Analyses, which is operated by the Franklin Institute of Philadelphia. Like the Rand operation, the Center for Naval Analyses is primarily concerned with placing at least an academic veneer on naval programs.

The Air Force has generally been the most open of the services in its lobbying, but the Army and the Navy also know how to organize their contractors and their supporters on Capitol Hill.

In 1961 the Army was pressing for early production of its Nike-Zeus antimissile missile (part of the family of missiles that was the subject of the Senate Investigations subcommittee's 1962 probe of profit-pyramiding among defense contractors). The weapon had not been tested to the satisfaction of the Defense Department, but the Army and Western Electric, the prime contractor for the project, put pressure for production of the missile on both Congress and the new Kennedy Administration, pledged to expand the nation's defense effort.

The campaign began with an issue of *Army* magazine featuring articles by generals praising the Nike-Zeus and advertisements by Western Electric and eight of the subcontractors for the project. The magazine is published by the Association of the United States Army, which, like the Air Force Association, is made up of military officers, retired officers, and defense contractors. The Nike-Zeus issue of *Army* contained a map showing that thirty-seven states were already sharing in the work and would get even more defense dollars once production began on a project that might cost $20 billion before it was completed.

Soon the Senate and House rang with speeches calling for Nike-Zeus production to start immediately. Senator B. Everett Jordan of North Carolina, Senator Frank Carlson of Kansas, Representative George P. Miller of California, and Representative Daniel J. Flood of Pennsylvania all spoke up for Nike-Zeus.

So did Representative John W. McCormack of Massachusetts, then Democratic leader in the House and now Speaker of the House. All of their states had contractors working on the project, but the congressional pressure was still not enough to get the Nike-Zeus into production. Despite the well-planned Army maneuver, Kennedy did not put Nike-Zeus on the production line.

The Army Association also prefers the Sheraton-Park Hotel for its annual conventions, which generally follow the Air Force Association meetings by a couple of months. But the 1964 Army Association convention was not the usual convivial gathering. The meeting came a few days before a new Defense Department regulation, prohibiting department employees from accepting "any favor, gratuity, or entertainment" from anyone doing business with the department, went into effect. The sixty to one hundred hospitality suites usually found at the Army Association conventions, and the AFA meetings, were missing from the Army gathering in 1964. Fifty of the 180 companies that generally buy tickets for Army officers who want to attend the Association's annual dinner withdrew their generosity when they discovered that the tickets would have to be given out only in the name of the Association rather than under the names of the individual defense contractors.

In the 1960's the Navy's most important engagement has been in defense of its antiquated and inefficient ship construction and repair yards. If Secretary McNamara could have brushed political considerations aside, several of the Navy yards would have been closed early in the Kennedy Administration. But it was not until November 1964 that McNamara was finally able to announce plans to close three of the yards.

Yet not even the Navy itself had been able to get a survey to show that its own yards are as efficient as those of private shipbuilders. When the private builders commissioned Ernst and Ernst to study comparative costs, the accounting firm found that work performed in Navy yards was from 20 to 28 percent more expensive than the same kind of work done by private firms. The Navy then ordered its own survey, which was made by Arthur Anderson and Company, another reputable accounting firm. Construction costs were reported by the Anderson company to be from 15 to 31 percent more expensive in Navy yards, repairs 10 percent higher, and modernization 8 percent higher.

Lobbying with and for the Navy are two powerful organizations, the Navy League and the National Security Industrial Association, the Navy's counterparts to the Air Force Association and the Association of the United States Army.

On Capitol Hill, the Navy's strongest supporter until his retirement in 1964 was Democratic Representative Carl Vinson of Georgia, who was chairman of the House Armed Services Committee from its establishment in 1947. Before the committee was set up under the Congressional Reorganization Act, Vinson headed the Naval Affairs Committee, where his energetic efforts on behalf of the Navy led his colleagues to refer to him, behind his back, as Admiral Vinson. Vinson was an autocrat who ran his committee as if he were the captain of an eighteenth century man-of-war.

A new-found congressional friend of the Navy is the Joint Committee on Atomic Energy, which in December 1963 issued a report extremely critical of Secretary McNamara for failing to order the installation of a nuclear power plant on a new aircraft carrier. McNamara argued that atomic power would be far more expensive than the use of conventional oil-fueled power plants and would provide no significant advances justifying the additional cost. The Joint Committee disputed his figures as well as his conclusions. The committee's position was not surprising because it has become the Capitol Hill advocate for the expanded use of nuclear power.

This, then, was the "jungle" in which McNamara found himself when he took over as Secretary of Defense in 1961. Each of the three services had become accustomed to doing much as it pleased, despite the hopes of the immediate post-World War II years that the new civilian-directed Defense Department would bring order and direction out of the Pentagon. Instead, the rivalries among the services had intensified. The congressional committees charged with overseeing the operations of the Defense Department became less and less effective and more and more the captives of the very services they were supposed to supervise. The influence of the defense contractors, the communities that had come to depend on defense work, the union members who realize that the bigger the defense program the more jobs there will be, and the businessmen who perform services for the defense workers, all became greater as military contracts became a way of life that seemed to millions of Americans to be permanent—and extremely comfortable.

McNamara, however, succeeded in establishing the civilian presence in the Pentagon where others had failed because, with the firm support of both President Kennedy and President Johnson, he has tried to make decisions on the basis of rational judgments rather than emotional arguments advanced by one or the other of the services.

This is what the disputes over the TFX airplane contract, the development of the B-70 or RS-70 plane, the cancellation of the Air Force's Skybolt missile and Dyna-Soar space projects, and the closing of over 500 obsolete but job-producing military bases have been about. McNamara also set up the Defense Supply Agency to centralize purchasing, and with the aid of computers he has sought to measure the effectiveness of new weapon concepts in terms of their costs, has tried to end the expensive and usually unnecessary "gold-plating" of weapons, and has injected more genuine competitive bidding in the awarding of defense contracts.

But despite McNamara's efforts to reduce costs, defense spending increased $6 billion from 1961 to 1964, in large part because of President Kennedy's desire to increase the nation's conventional fighting forces, which he felt had been neglected with the emphasis on nuclear weapons during the Eisenhower Administration.

"My problem," McNamara said in testimony in 1963 before the House Defense Appropriations subcommittee, "has been to prevent appropriations exceeding those which we have recommended. There have been tremendous pressures, for example, to appropriate funds for programs that I do not believe add to our national security: . . . pressures to appropriate funds for such missile systems as Skybolt, which we do not require to achieve the appropriate level of nuclear deterrence; pressures to carry out development of aircraft programs such as the RS-70, which are not necessary to our national security; pressures to add to the funds for such development projects as Dyna-Soar beyond the limits which we can properly and effectively spend."

McNamara and his civilian aides have been the only force in Washington trying to throttle the military-industrial complex. McNamara has not hesitated to incur the wrath of the services by cutting off some of their pet projects, but political considerations have prevented him from going as far as he would have liked. Even so, he reduced the 1964 defense budget by $13 billion and the 1965 budget by $10 billion before submitting them to Congress.

During the House Defense Appropriations subcommittee's 1964 hearings, chairman George H. Mahon, a Democrat from Texas who is now chairman of the full Appropriations Committee, said to McNamara: "There have been statements made that Secretary McNamara is a tremendous man with great ability, but that he is taking unto himself the making of so many decisions, and he is providing such strong leadership that leadership probably is not being otherwise developed in the services. It is said that if Robert McNamara would always be Secretary of Defense, this would not be bad, but that when McNamara leaves the department and we get an ordinary garden variety of Secretary of Defense, we are going to get into trouble."

McNamara replied with a statement that well summarizes his view of the enormous problems in the Defense Department.

"Let me simply say," McNamara began, "that if one is to avoid waste resulting from interservice rivalry, then the Secretary of Defense must make decisions which, by definition, are contrary to the recommendations of one or another of the individual services. . . .

"The basic objective of the management system we are introducing and trying to operate is the establishment of a rational, as opposed to an emotional, foundation for the decisions we must make, as to what size force and what type of force the country will maintain. This rational structure, this intellectual foundation for determining the military forces we should build and support, is something that is laid out on paper. It is laid out first as an analysis of the potential contingency war plans for a variety of situations and, then, as a translation of those war plans into military forces. And finally, the force structure must be translated into programs and budgets. There is no reason in the world why this system cannot be continued in the future. As a matter of fact, I think it must be; and I think, if the executive branch does not continue it, Congress itself can force a continuation. . . .

"The cost effectiveness study is applicable when we are trying to decide to buy aircraft A or aircraft B, one having a ten mile per hour advantage over the other at a specific cost increase.

"The basic question is, 'Should we have either one of them?' To determine whether we should have either aircraft, and to determine whether we should have one hundred or two hundred or one thousand of them requires a rather sophisticated analysis of the potential threat and of our potential responses to it under a variety of circumstances. When I say we are trying to establish a rational foundation for our military forces, I am thinking of exactly this kind of analysis."

In his discussion of these basic problems and his approach to them, McNamara also pointed out that "in adding to a defense program as large as the one we now have, we soon encounter the law of diminishing returns; each additional increment of resources used produces a proportionately smaller increment of overall defense capability. While the benefits to be gained from each additional increment cannot be measured with precision, careful cost-effectiveness analyses can greatly assist in eliminating those program proposals which clearly contribute little to our military strength in terms of the costs involved."

McNamara's attempts to apply rational analyses to proposed weapons and his efforts to avoid duplication have extended even to the development of complicated equipment like the TFX airplane (the initials stand for tactical fighter, experimental), which in 1963 was the subject of a year-long study by the Senate Investigations subcommittee headed by Senator McClellan. Over the protests of both the Navy and the Air Force, McNamara ordered the development of an advanced fighter plane that would meet the maneuverability and range specifications sought by both services. McNamara overrode the decisions of military selection boards and awarded the $6.5 billion contract for the TFX to General Dynamics rather than to Boeing. This decision was based on McNamara's belief that General Dynamics would be able to build the plane more efficiently than could Boeing even though Boeing's cost estimates were lower. Boeing had greatly exceeded its cost estimates on some defense contracts in the past, and McNamara feared this would again be the case with the TFX project. McNamara also felt that General Dynamics better understood the commonalty approach he was emphasizing. By this, McNamara meant the interchangeability of parts between planes built for the Air Force and those delivered to the Navy. The allegations that the real reason for awarding the contract to General Dynamics was that it was a Texas firm with important political connections in

Washington were never proved during the course of the long Senate investigation.

If the Navy and the Air Force had each been allowed to produce its own plane, two production lines and two pipelines of spare parts and other support equipment would have had to have been set up. As it is, the Pentagon's huge inventory of more than 4 million items is crammed with extra parts for servicing the great variety of airplanes maintained by the Navy and the Air Force. Many of the airplanes perform substantially the same missions and vary only slightly in design.

In fact, the Air Force and the Navy have so much unnecessary equipment that they cannot keep track of it. In 1963, the GAO reported that $147 million worth of equipment had disappeared from the Navy's records while the Air Force had "lost" $164 million worth.

Most members of Congress did not, however, look on the TFX contract as a gigantic effort to bring some order and savings out of the costly defense program. To the senators and representatives, the TFX contract meant jobs and profits, and a lot of both.

Secretary of the Air Force Zuckert told the Senate Investigations subcommittee of the procession of senators and representatives who talked to him about the advantages of doing some of the TFX work in their states, but he insisted that their interest in the TFX contract did not influence him. Nevertheless the senators and representatives did not think they were simply passing the time of day as they visited or telephoned Zuckert in 1962, when the competition between Boeing and General Dynamics was at its height.

From Oklahoma came the late Senator Robert S. Kerr, Senator Mike Monroney, and Representative Carl Albert, the House Democratic leader. They, Monroney said later, simply wanted to remind Zuckert of the idle government-owned aircraft plant in Tulsa that had been operated by the Douglas Company.

From Missouri came Senator Stuart Symington, who had been the first Secretary of the Air Force, and the late Representative Clarence Cannon, who was a crusty and powerful chairman of the House Appropriations Committee, to argue for the McDonnell Aircraft Corporation in St. Louis. From Texas came Representative Joe M. Kilgore to press General Dynamics' case. From Kansas came Republican Senators Frank Carlson and James B. Pearson and Representative Garner E. Shriver to extol the merits of Boeing's extensive facilities at Wichita.

Also arguing for Boeing, which has its headquarters in Seattle, were Washington's two Democratic senators, Warren G. Magnuson and Henry M. Jackson. A letter came in from Representative Vinson, who was concerned about the Lockheed plant in his state of Georgia.

Unlike most of the members of Congress who sought to influence Zuckert in his recommendations to McNamara, one lone Texan made no excuses on the grounds of public interest for his intensive lobbying. Jim Wright, representing Fort Worth, where General Dynamics has been doing most of its work on the TFX contract, told the House in 1963: "In the absence of a substantial contract of this type, the General Dynamics team at Fort Worth was faced with dismemberment. . . . It meant the difference between employment or unemployment for thousands of my constituents. . . . Let me be completely frank. . . . I talked about this subject with everybody . . . I could get to listen . . . both military and civilian officials. . . . That does not in my judgment amount to undesirable political influence. The same sort of thing was being attempted by the other side."

McNamara is not only the first Secretary of Defense to have tried to base both strategic and procurement decisions on rational rather than emotional grounds, he also is the first to have followed through on plans to reduce costs. His three-point cost-cutting program has been designed (1) to buy only what is needed; (2) to buy at the lowest price whenever possible and (3) to reduce operating costs by ending unnecessary operations and by standardizing and consolidating operations.

Commenting on McNamara's efforts to reduce costs, Democratic Senator Paul H. Douglas of Illinois, a long-time critic of Pentagon waste, said in the fall of 1964: "From 1950 to 1960 I tried to cut military waste. I believed that $2 to $3 billion a year could be saved by unifying the supply systems of the three separate services, by more competitive bidding, by better buying and disposal of surplus items. I had almost no success during this entire period. In 1960 I exposed a number of horrible examples, but the Defense Department responded by denying that any problem existed. At one time they had dozens of officers and civilian personnel in my office looking at the items. They spent hundreds of man-hours and thousands of dollars trying to disprove them. However, they failed. When Secretary McNamara was appointed, I wrote to him outlining our recommendations for reform. About every six months since then I have met with him, and from the beginning he has acted. The result is that this year we have saved $2.5 billion, and reforms have been put into effect which will ultimately save $4.5 billion. Persistence has finally brought great savings to the public in a fight which often seemed hopeless."

In discussing the Pentagon's new efforts to buy only what is needed, McNamara noted in a report submitted to President Johnson in the summer of 1964 that the Defense Department carries 4 million items in its inventories, and indicated that past excesses in purchasing had resulted in the accumulation of $10 billion worth of surplus stocks. "Once we overbuy," McNamara said, "we not only spend money on inventories which are never used, but we also set in motion a whole train of unnecessary expenditures—for more warehouses, more transportation, and more personnel—ending years later with large surpluses which the government has to sell for approximately seven cents on the dollar." From 1958 through 1962 sales of surplus military equipment disposed of from $4 to $8 billion worth of material each year.

McNamara went on to say that in the 1963 fiscal year, planned purchases were reduced by $700 million because of a constant review of what was needed and that in 1964 these kinds of reductions amounted to $1.4 billion.

McNamara said that an existing gyroscope for Polaris submarines was improved at a saving of $44 million over the cost of a new instrument, and that the M-12 machine gun was found to be as useful as the more costly M-85 on most Army combat vehicles, saving $21 million. Other savings resulted from Air Force studies showing that the storage life of the solid propellant motor for the Minuteman missile could be increased from three to four years at an immediate annual reduction in costs of $25 million; from Navy investigations that reduced aircraft engine requirements by 297 units at a cost reduction of $3.2 million; and from Army studies of insect-repellent needs which cut costs by $1.2 million.

New uses are also being found for materials in surplus stock. Powder from three types of surplus Army projectiles was reblended for use in a 175 mm projectile, at a saving of $5.1 million. The Navy saved $6.1 million by recovering silver from dental clinics, old batteries, and X-ray films for reuse in making batteries for torpedoes. The Marine Corps obtained 114,000 projectiles it needed from excess Army stocks and thus saved $10.7 million. The Defense Supply Agency modified excess trousers to meet new requirements at a saving of $452,000.

Other savings have been achieved in the elimination of gold-plating (unnecessarily high quality standards that add little or nothing to safety and performance standards). McNamara estimated that the savings in this area totaled $119 million. By eliminating and consolidating items in the Defense Department's huge inventories, nearly half a million separate items were discontinued and $50 million was saved.

In his efforts to get the services to buy only at the lowest possible price, McNamara went on to note in his report, he has been able to increase the number of items purchased through competitive bidding while decreasing the number of cost-plus-fixed-fee contracts. Under such contracts a company is guaranteed all of its costs on a defense project as well as a fee for its services, so there is little or no incentive for efficiency. Along with his program for cutting down on the number of such contracts, McNamara has sought to introduce what he calls "greater risk-sharing by contractors in the development and production of complex weapons and equipment."

The number of contracts awarded on the basis of competitive bidding did increase, as McNamara noted, from 33 percent of all defense contracts in 1961 to 40 percent in 1964; but as Senator Douglas' Subcommittee on Defense Procurement of the Joint Congressional Economic Committee pointed out in its 1964 report on the economic impact of the defense program, negotiated bids still accounted for 87 percent of the total value of defense contracts, which is a much more meaningful figure than the one used by McNamara. As both McNamara and the Joint Economic Committee report noted, competitive procurement saves an average of twenty-five cents on the dollar.

As part of his effort to break up the close relationships that have developed between the services and their contractors (constituting a key element in the military-industrial complex that former President Eisenhower warned against), McNamara has tried to force the services to divide new weapons into their component parts as soon as possible after development so that competitive bids can be sought on each part. The individualistic Admiral Rickover demonstrated the feasibility of this method some years ago—even in constructing the most sophisticated equipment—when he directed that work on the atomic submarines be split up so that competitive bids could be obtained and knowledge of this new technology could be more widely spread.

McNamara has significantly reduced the number of cost-plus-fixed-fee-contracts. In 1952 these amounted to only 13 percent of the value of all defense contracts. By 1961 they had increased to 38 percent of the total.

In 1961 McNamara set as his goal the reduction of cost-plus-fixed-fee contracts to no more than 12 percent of all contracts by the end of the 1965 fiscal year. He achieved this goal a year earlier than he had planned, shifting an average of $5.5 billion in contracts in each of three years to fixed-price and price-incentive formulas. He estimated that these shifts saved the government at least 10 percent of the cost of carrying out the contracts, or half a billion dollars a year. The shift, McNamara also reported, led to more detailed and more advance planning of programs, projects, and the execution of contracts, all of which have contributed to more efficient production and the saving of money.

"A recent case," said McNamara, "is the contract for the Vela satellite, used to detect nuclear detonations in space, in which the contractor's incentive fee was based on a number of performance factors including the length of time the vehicle performed satisfactorily in orbit. As a result of the spectacular length of life of the first launch, the Air Force was able to reduce the total program cost 32 percent—a saving of $26 million. The contractor earned $115,000 in additional fees."

McNamara has been stressing the need for careful writing of contracts like the one for the Vela satellite to provide for greater profits to the efficient company—and smaller profits, or no profits at all, perhaps even losses, for the company that fails to live up to its promises. But, as McNamara has discovered, it is not an easy job to change habits to which the armed services and their contractors have become accustomed over the years.

The third part of McNamara's cost-reduction program has been the most controversial from both a political and economic standpoint because it involves the closing of bases and other military installations. Not only do old Army forts, venerable Navy yards, and even Air Force fields that are only as old as World War II become an accepted part of community life, they are also part of a community's industrial complex. They are counted on for permanent jobs and profits that often provide an extremely important part of a community's economic livelihood.

To his credit, McNamara has been able to carry out to a considerable degree his ambitious plans formulated early in the Kennedy Administration to close down large numbers of obsolete bases. In his July 1964 report to Johnson, McNamara noted that a total of 556 actions had been taken since 1961 to close bases or to consolidate and reduce operations. These actions, McNamara added, resulted in the elimination of 81,600 jobs and in annual savings of $568 million.

In November 1964 McNamara ordered the closing or curtailing of another ninety-five installations—including the New York Navy Yard in Brooklyn and the Portsmouth Navy Yard in New Hampshire. Two other Navy yards, San Francisco and Mare Island in California, were consolidated into one operation. McNamara estimated that all of these 1964 actions would eliminate 63,401 jobs and save the government an additional $477 million a year in defense operating expenditures.

Adding McNamara's 1964 actions to his previous base-closing decisions, the claimed savings amount to more than $1 billion a year and the cutback in employment to more than 145,000 jobs. However, McNamara stressed, all of the civilian employees whose jobs were eliminated since 1961 were offered other positions in the Defense Department. McNamara also assured the affected communities that the government would give them all the assistance at its command.

When McNamara made public the 1964 base closings at a press conference just two weeks after election day, he denied that the timing of the announcements had anything to do with the elections. He steadfastly maintained that the decisions on the closing of the bases simply were not ready for announcement before the third week in November. He also said that this was the time of year these announcements are usually made. (McNamara did announce the closing of a group of bases in December 1963, but that was the only precedent.) Finally, he denied that political considerations play any part in his decisions.

Whether politics was a consideration or not in the selection of the bases to be closed, McNamara convinced few persons in Washington that the timing for the announcement was not deliberately set for after the elections to try to minimize its political impact.

Another controversial part of McNamara's cost-cutting efforts is the Defense Supply Agency, which the Secretary set up in 1962 to centralize the purchasing of common supplies and equipment needed by all of the services. The mere establishment of a unified supply agency was a triumph. Ever since the Defense Department was created at the end of World War II in an attempt to unify the efforts of the services, a central supply agency has been bitterly fought by the admirals and the generals, many of whom are bent on preserving the identities, peculiarities, and rivalries of their service at whatever the cost to the taxpayer. Whenever a unified supply agency was mentioned, dark and foreboding words were muttered in the Pentagon about a "fourth service."

But nothing of the sort has happened. In its first three years the agency took over the purchasing and management of 1.6 million of the 4 million separate items that the services feel they must have to meet the requirements of modern warfare. The agency is already saving taxpayers $55 million a year as it cuts its way through the procurement jungle in the Pentagon. A prime concern of the new agency is the elimination of the duplication of supplies and supply lines. In the past one service frequently sold for scrap what another needed and was buying.

"We have now turned our attention to a new area," McNamara said in discussing the Defense Supply Agency in his July 1964 report to the President. "On June 4, 1964, I directed the establishment of a single organization to manage the 150 field offices and 20,000 personnel concerned with the administration of defense contracts after their award, including material inspection, production expediting, industrial security, payment of contractor invoices, and a variety of related functions. Responsibility for organizing this new effort over the next two years has been assigned to the Defense Supply Agency. Substantial economies—now estimated at $60 million annually— are expected to result from this consolidation."

In concluding his report to the President, McNamara said that "savings of $2.5 billion were realized in FY [fiscal year] 1964—65 percent more than estimated one year ago," that defense contractors as well as Defense Department officials and military officers were helping to make the cost-cutting program succeed, and that his cost-reduction target of $4.6 billion a year by 1968 would be reached.

Unfortunately for McNamara and the taxpayers, however, there has been no significant net reduction in defense spending or federal expenditures in general resulting from his cost-cutting efforts. Total annual defense expenditures remain in the $50 billion range because of the cost of highly sophisticated weapons, pay increases voted by Congress for both military officers and civilian employees of the Defense Department, and a host of other reasons. Nevertheless, defense costs would be even higher than they now are if it were not for McNamara's strenuous efforts.

But have McNamara's cost-reduction efforts cut so deeply that they have gone through Pentagon fat and into military sinew and muscle? And has McNamara's very willingness to make decisions greatly damaged the morale of military officers and thus harmed the nation's defenses?

"You cannot make decisions simply by asking yourself whether something might be nice to have," McNamara told the American Society of Newspaper Editors, meeting in Washington in the spring of 1963. "You have to make a judgment on how much is enough. I emphasize judgment because you can't even be sure yourself, much less prove to others, that your decision was precisely right to the last dollar—even to the last billion dollars. But the decision has to be made.

"The Secretary of Defense," McNamara added, "and I am talking about any Secretary of Defense, must make certain kinds of decisions, not because he presumes his judgment to be superior to his advisers, military or civilian, but because his position is the best place from which to make those decisions."

One of the most forceful challenges to McNamara's point of view and decisiveness came in a speech delivered by Admiral George Anderson to the National Press Club in Washington shortly after he retired in the summer of 1963 from the Navy as Chief of Naval Operations.

"I am gravely concerned," said Anderson, "that within the Department of Defense there is not the degree of confidence and trust between the civilian and military echelons that the importance of their common objective requires. This two-way responsibility requires wisdom, respect, and understanding from both sides. Uniformed personnel know that they must be continually responsive to national security requirements. They must also be responsive to any particular form of administrative civilian authority prevailing in the Department at any particular time and to the statutory responsibilities of their service secretaries. Civilian officials and staff assistants should recognize that forceful expression of contrary views in proper channels or frank response to congressional inquiry do not represent a challenge to the valid concept of civilian control. . . .

"I am concerned also," Anderson continued, "regarding a trend in the major procurement policies within the Department of Defense to the ultimate detriment of our military services. One proposal has been advanced which would in effect eliminate the requirement for specific recommendations by military personnel on matters such as design competitions or source selection procedures. I view any diminution of military recommendations on weapons procurement with grave alarm. . . . .

"There is a myth to the effect that historically the generals and admirals, the colonels and the captains, are villains opposed to progress, and refugees from new ideas. On the contrary, history shows that daring ideas from the military often have been ignored: Colonel Charles de Gaulle in his ignored warning on the dangers of the Maginot Line type of defense; Admiral James O. Richardson in his caution against leaving the fleet exposed at Pearl Harbor. William S. Sims, as a young lieutenant before World War I, took his daring case for gunnery reform directly to the President. Admirals Moffett and Towers pressed forward with the development of United States naval aviation to the enhancement of our naval power. Generals MacArthur, Billy Mitchell, and 'Hap' Arnold, and Admiral Mahan were daring, original, and creative as were Admirals Rickover and Raborn in engineering Polaris breakthroughs. All belie this myth that the military are not progressive. . . .

"There is another alarming peril to obscuring the role of the military, found in a modern fallacy that theories or computers or economics or numbers of weapons win wars. Alone, they do not. Good leadership unfailingly recognizes that man is the key to success or failure."

Anderson's views reflect the misgivings most military men have had about McNamara's assertion of the authority of the Secretary of Defense and his civilian aides. It is really a question of who should be charged with making the final decisions

—the Joint Chiefs of Staff, the Secretary of Defense, the President, or the Armed Services Committees on Capitol Hill. And whoever makes these decisions must of course constantly be aware of all the pressures and different points of view bearing on the decisions. It does, however, seem best to centralize the decision-making process in the hands of the Secretary of Defense and the President rather than to leave it in limbo, as in so many instances during the 1950's.

The defense program is indeed so filled with imponderables that no one can say with any finality that enough is being spent on defense to make the nation impregnable—or whether the money that is being expended is being used in the most effective way possible. Most generals and admirals feel they never have enough. There is always the natural desire for a little extra, a little additional protection here or there.

But somewhere the proliferation of defenses and weapons must stop, if perhaps only temporarily while the nation takes stock of what it has built and decides whether it has in fact constructed an adequate defense or whether still more is needed.

The dimensions of the problem can be better understood by looking at a part of the defense program that was boldly turned into a subsidy for the United States mining industry during the 1950's. This is the stockpile of strategic materials, now valued at more than $8 billion and much larger than the nation could possibly use in any kind of war. Yet it is proving all but impossible to reduce the size of this stockpile because of the many interests with a stake in its present size and because of a shocking lack of advance planning to offset the economic and political consequences of its reduction.

CHAPTER 6

The Ever-Growing Stockpile

"I WAS astonished," President Kennedy told a press conference early in 1962, "to find that the total stockpile now amounts to $7.7 billion worth of materials, an amount that exceeds the total inventory of farm products and, of more importance, an amount that exceeds our emergency requirements . . . by nearly $3.4 billion."

The late President's astonishment led to the first investigation of the stockpiles of strategic and critical materials that the United States has been accumulating since the end of World War II. The purchase and storage of the materials began after Congress approved the Strategic and Critical Materials Stockpiling Act of 1946. The purpose of the legislation, and of similar laws passed during the Korean War, was to assure that the United States would always have on hand ample supplies of materials that would be needed in time of war but might not be readily available through the normal channels of trade.

When the first stockpiling legislation was approved by Congress within a year after the end of World War II, there was general agreement on Capitol Hill and in the Truman Administration that such a program was needed. Natural rubber and other materials considered necessary to the successful prosecution of a war had been in short supply during World War II. In 1938 and 1939 Congress had authorized the Navy and the Army to acquire limited stocks of such strategic materials as chromite, quartz crystals, rubber, and tin, but the amounts of the materials purchased were small and inadequate to American needs once the United States entered the war.

Despite the experience before World War II the stockpile grew slowly in the late 1940's. By the time the United States found itself in the Korean War in the summer of 1950, only $1.6 billion worth of materials had been accumulated.

But in the five years immediately after the end of the Korean War, the stockpile grew enormously until in 1958 a total of $7.3 billion worth of materials had been accumulated. By 1962, as President Kennedy noted, the size of the stockpile had increased still further and was valued at $7.7 billion. As Kennedy also noted, the cost to the government of acquiring the materials had totaled $8.9 billion.

The stockpile that grew so fast in the 1950's included such materials as aluminum, asbestos, bauxite, chromite, cobalt, copper, diamonds, feathers, fluorspar, graphite, iodine, lead, magnesium, manganese, mercury, mica, molybdenum, nickel, platinum, quartz, rubber, rubies, sapphires, shellac, silk, sperm oil, tin, tungsten, vanadium, and zinc. In all, there were 46 million tons of ninety-eight different materials stored at 213 locations throughout the country, and it was costing the government $292 million a year just to store the materials.

All of the stockpiling had been carried out in considerable secrecy throughout the 1950's. The stockpiling legislation provided that most of the decisions concerning the size and composition of the stockpile be kept from the public in the interest of national security.

The secrecy surrounding the program was stripped away during an investigation of it in 1962 and 1963 by the National Stockpile and Naval Petroleum Reserves subcommittee of the

Senate Armed Services Committee. The subcommittee was headed by Democratic Senator Stuart Symington of Missouri.

The subcommittee's hearings and its report on them, issued in the fall of 1963, revealed situations that are central to any discussion of the politics and economics of the defense program and the problems associated with a decline in defense spending. The political overtones that clouded the subcommittee's investigation were another indication of the problems involved in shutting off defense programs. Although the subcommittee's report was made public, it was never officially filed as a Senate document because of squabbling among subcommittee members over the report's criticism of members of President Eisenhower's Cabinet.

The stockpile of strategic materials grew far beyond the nation's needs in large part because of changing estimates of those needs as well as because of decisions taken during the 1950's to change the purpose of some of the stockpiling. As in the case of so many other defense programs, needs other than those of the military were taken into consideration in determining stockpiling goals. Yet, so accustomed have Americans become to waste in the name of defense that little has been done to solve the stockpiling problems in the months since the Symington investigation ended late in 1963.

The story of the lead and zinc stockpile is perhaps the best illustration of the way the stockpile program was used for purposes other than defense.

The mining of lead and zinc has been a declining industry in the United States since the end of World War II. Many of the best mines have been exhausted, and most of the remaining deposits of lead and zinc are expensive and difficult to develop for commercial use. There are, however, still large deposits of lead and zinc in Canada, Mexico, and other countries, and the foreign metals began to find a ready market in the United States early in the 1950's during the Korean War.

The increased demand for lead and zinc as a result of the Korean War provided some temporary relief for the domestic mining industry, but when the war ended in 1953 lead and zinc production in the United States suffered another setback. Fortunately for the industry, however, it had friends in important places in the government.

Until 1954 stockpiling goals were supposed to be established by using a single, standardized method. The military would determine its wartime requirements for a material. To these requirements would be added the essential needs of the civilian economy during wartime. For the purposes of setting the level of these requirements, it was assumed that a war would last five years and that a five-year supply of the strategic materials should be readily available at all times. If the domestic supplies of a material as well as supplies that could be obtained with some assurance from foreign countries during wartime did not add up to the five-year needs, stockpiling of the material was authorized. The stockpiling goal was generally the difference between the available supplies and the amount needed to fight a five-year war. But the program was never administered according to the regulations written for it.

"The original objectives for most materials in the national stockpile were established in 1944," the Symington subcommittee noted in its report. "In most instances these objectives were arbitrarily established by resorting to the total consumption of the United States in 1943, a peak year in the consumption of materials as we were then engaged in a world war, and subtracting therefrom the expected supply and multiplying the result by five. . . .

"But the hearings have disclosed," the report continued, "that from the very outset objectives were not established by uniform methods. . . . The first objective in zinc established in 1944 was also arrived at by multiplying the 1943 consumption less supply by five. However, the supply was so large that the result was an excess of 382,000 tons. The supply was arbitrarily decreased by one half to discount an expected depletion in reserves over twenty years. . . . This created a deficit of 1,500,000 tons, which became the objective. The first objective in lead was 1,100,000 tons. It was based on the 1943 consumption less supply multiplied by five, with a discount of 25 percent for depletion of reserves over twenty years. . . . The first objective in nickel was set by multiplying the 1943 consumption less supply by five and subtracting supplies from New Caledonia and Canada."

The goals for the lead and zinc stockpiles outlined in the subcommittee report remained substantially the same until 1954 when at the direction of President Eisenhower the Office of Defense Mobilization set up two objectives for determining stockpiling goals for all strategic materials. One was called a basic objective and the other a maximum objective. The basic objective was the goal that had been previously set by balancing requirements against available supplies for a five-year period. The new, maximum objective could be determined through one of two methods. Under one system all foreign supplies beyond North America would be discounted because of the danger that all ocean transport would be cut off in wartime. "This resulted in most instances," the subcommittee report pointed out, "in the establishment of a maximum objective which was substantially larger than the objective then prevailing."

The second method of determining the new, maximum objective was by basing wartime goals on one year's normal use by the entire economy of the material in question. "This," said the subcommittee, "became known as the one-year rule and was applicable to all minerals but was actually employed only in the case of lead and zinc in setting objectives. This was later reduced to six months' use of industry in the United States in periods of active demand.

"It may be," the report continued, "that the very nature of the materials under consideration prevented the use of uniform methods in setting objectives. However, the wielding of wide discretionary power in this respect leads to an abuse in the setting of objectives, especially where the power is exercised in secrecy, as in the operation of the stockpile."

The lead and zinc purchases under the new criteria began in June 1954, after a special Cabinet committee had declared that a healthy and efficient lead and zinc mining industry in the United States producing at a high level each year was necessary to provide an adequate mobilization base for the industry. Members of the special Cabinet Committee on Minerals Policy were Secretary of State John Foster Dulles, Secretary of Commerce Sinclair Weeks, Secretary of the Interior Douglas McKay, and Arthur S. Flemming, director of the Office of Defense Mobilization. Secretary of the Treasury George M. Humphrey was an adviser to the committee.

The Symington subcommittee reported that Felix E. Wormser, Assistant Secretary of the Interior for Mineral Resources, "did much of the groundwork of preparing information in developing the program" for the purchase of lead and zinc. Before becoming Assistant Secretary, Wormser was vice president of the St. Joseph Lead Company, the largest producer of lead in the United States. At the end of the Eisenhower Administration, Wormser returned to St. Joseph Lead where he became a vice president again.

Although the new purchase program for lead and zinc started in June 1954, it did not move into high gear until the following August when President Eisenhower rejected on foreign policy grounds the industry's plea for increases in import duties to protect it from foreign production.

"I am," Eisenhower announced, "directing the Director of the Office of Defense Mobilization to increase purchases at market prices of newly mined domestic lead and zinc, under the long-term stockpile program. The government is in a position where it could purchase in the fiscal year up to 200,000 tons of lead and 300,000 tons of zinc."

For five years, from 1954 through 1958, the purchases of lead and zinc authorized by Eisenhower were continued. The government paid a total of $204 million for 751,000 pounds of lead and zinc that it did not need. Two producers, St. Joseph Lead and American Smelting and Refining Company, supplied the government with 85 percent of the lead. Four producers sold the government 69 percent of the zinc it bought. They were American Zinc Sales, Anaconda, American Smelting and Refining, and St. Joseph Lead.

Four times during the five-year period, the base year to be used in determining the size of the lead and zinc stockpiles was changed. It started out as 1953 but then was shifted to 1955, a year of record high automobile production and record high use of lead and zinc. Further changes in the base periods were made in 1957 and 1958.

"Government employees most intimately connected with the fixing of lead-zinc objectives," the Symington subcommittee reported, "testified under oath that they were instructed to find the highest years of consumption in order to continue purchases of lead and zinc; that such purchases had no relation to the security needs of the United States; that such an obvious waste of the taxpayers' money had a demoralizing effect on the ODM [Office of Defense Mobilization] staff which consistently recommended against this unnecessary spending."

The subcommittee found that for at least thirty-six months the government's purchases of lead and zinc for its stockpiles "succeeded admirably in its purpose of raising and supporting lead-zinc prices." The subcommittee report said that the program was able to put a floor under prices because purchases were made monthly and were paid for in cash. They were allocated among lead and zinc producers on the basis of their share of the market in 1952. In 1954 government purchases of both lead and zinc amounted to more than 40 percent of total domestic production and remained a substantial part of production throughout the five-year program.

All of these purchases and manipulations of goals were carried on despite a March 1954 directive from the Office of

Defense Mobilization, which cautioned: "Stockpile funds shall not be used for the primary purpose of engaging in economic warfare, of developing new sources of supply, of stabilizing markets, or for any other such economic operation, domestic or foreign."

In the long run, however, the program failed in its objective of helping lead and zinc mining companies and their employees to provide a permanent floor under the industry's prices. After three years lead and zinc prices in the United States were so good that foreign imports again began to flood the country, threatening the entire price structure that had been built up so carefully and at such cost to the government.

In its report on the expensive lead and zinc purchases that were made in the name of the nation's defenses, the Symington subcommittee summed up the situation in these words:

"With such a large part of domestic-mined production being locked up in the stockpile and purchases being made on a noncompetitive basis for a period of four years, the market necessarily rose until large quantities of foreign material had made a competitive impact upon the United States market. . . .

"When the artificial stimulus of the price support program raised domestic market prices, foreign low-cost materials flooded the market and actually destroyed any possible mobilization base in lead and zinc. Since the stockpile could not continue forever to support the lead and zinc industry, the domestic purchase programs were terminated and prices dropped to low levels which still prevail. . . .

"Regardless of the question of responsibility, the evil of the price support program was that it loaded the stockpile with great quantities of unneeded materials at a time when the Defense Department was seeking funds for more urgent defense needs. In addition, the manipulation of the free market system resulted in a dramatic price rise which forced the consuming public to pay higher prices to subsidize a particular industry. This was done without public knowledge under a cloak of secrecy imposed because of the supposed demands of national security . . ."

While the Office of Defense Mobilization was increasing stockpile goals for lead and zinc, it was allowing the domestic copper industry to postpone deliveries to the stockpile because this would help companies mining copper to take advantage of unexpected price increases.

In 1954 copper was considered to be one of the most critical of the materials being stockpiled by the government. Many contracts had been negotiated by the government and copper producers, calling for the delivery of specific quantities of metal every three months. The government had also signed contracts for the purchase of copper that were designed to encourage companies to maintain their production because copper was considered to be such an essential material in time of war.

Late in 1954, however, strikes in the copper mines of Southern Rhodesia, which has some of the richest deposits of the metal in the world, resulted in a temporary shortage of copper. Prices increased, and American producers of copper asked the Eisenhower Administration if they could postpone their deliveries to the government to take advantage of the higher prices on the open market. Administration officials agreed to the postponements sought by the companies. The companies were then able to realize what the Symington subcommittee called windfall profits of as much as nineteen cents per pound of copper. The government contract prices ranged from twenty-seven to thirty-two cents a pound while the market prices for copper during the period of world shortages were from thirty to forty-six cents a pound. The worldwide shortages continued from 1954 through 1955 and into 1956.

A total of 147,548,000 pounds of copper contracted for by the government for delivery to the stockpile was sold instead by industry directly in the open market. One result of this diversion was that deliveries to the stockpile were up to thirty months late. Another result was an increase in profits to the copper companies involved of $8,553,703.

"It is evident," commented the Symington subcommittee, "that once the government has embarked upon a plan of making large-scale purchases of strategic materials for stockpiling purposes, anything the government does to enforce or to forgive contracts for the delivery of such materials will have an impact on the market. ... Whatever one's concept of government participation in business may be, it is difficult to understand how once our government has entered into contracts for the purchase of large quantities of commodities, there is any other course for the government to follow than to protect its rights under the contracts to the fullest."

Lead, zinc, and copper were not the only commodities given special consideration by the government officials in charge of the stockpiling program. Another favored metal was molybdenum, which is used as an alloy in the manufacture of steel. Ninety percent of the free world's supply of molybdenum is located in the United States.

The Climax Molybdenum Company, which markets nearly all of the molybdenum produced in the United States and also dominates the world market for the metal, negotiated a contract with the government providing for deliveries over a period of several years. The price was set at the actual cost of production plus a fixed figure for amortization expenses and a profit of eighteen cents a pound. A ceiling of $1.07 a pound was placed on production costs.

The government contracted for a total of 50 million pounds of molybdenum, but in September 1955, the Climax Company was permitted to postpone deliveries to the government even though only 7,421,000 pounds of molybdenum had been placed in the stockpile. Climax wanted to divert its supplies of molybdenum to industrial markets because the demand for the metal had increased and prices had gone up on the open market.

"Climax," the Symington subcommittee report concluded, "was permitted to sell on the market rather than deliver to the stockpile on the ground that it was more vital to national defense to relieve domestic shortages than to meet the stockpile goal. The fact is, however, that Climax was using some of the diverted molybdenum to fill overseas orders. . . . During the period Climax was permitted to divert from the stockpile, its exports of molybdenum substantially increased and then dropped off sharply when the diversions were concluded. . . . Therefore, not only did Climax reap windfalls at the expense of the government, but the contract was finally canceled for a sum substantially less than the windfall profits accruing to the contractor by such cancellation."

The subcommittee estimated that the Climax Company was able to realize at least $4.5 million in additional profits by canceling its stockpiling contract after paying the government only $1.2 million for allowing the company to terminate its deliveries.

Still another indication of the political and economic orientation of the stockpiling program was the failure of the Office of Defense Mobilization to change its stockpiling goals until four years after the military had decided that planning should be based on the probability of a war lasting no longer than three years rather than the five-year period established at the end of World War II. The military shifted its planning from a five-year to a three-year base in 1954, but the stockpile objectives were not changed to the three-year base until 1958 despite Defense Department efforts to get the Office of Defense Mobilization to do so as early as 1955.

In August 1955, Assistant Secretary of Defense T. P. Pike wrote Arthur S. Flemming, the director of ODM, urging the adoption of planning goals based on the probability of a three-year war. Pike noted that if this change were made, some of the funds being used to stockpile supplies could be better spent on other defense needs.

But Flemming did not find Pike's arguments convincing, and the stockpile goals remained the same for another three years. Assistant Secretary of the Interior Wormser took Flemming's point of view in a letter he wrote to him in the summer of 1955.

"For one thing," said Wormser, "I believe a change in the five-year period would be considered a breach of faith by the mining industry in the light of the report of the President's Cabinet Committee on Mineral Policy published only a few months ago. I think the miners would have strong justification for resentment over the sudden change in policy. The most important declaration in the report of the Cabinet committee was the emphasis upon a strong, vigorous, and efficient domestic mining industry being essential to the prosperity of the nation. Therefore, unless we are prepared at the time any curtailment of stockpiling is contemplated to propose an alternate means of sustaining our mobilization base and to foster a healthy mining industry, this Administration is apt to find itself in unpleasant and, I may say, well-deserved political difficulties."

The Eisenhower Administration did not have to face these political unpleasantries. Later in 1955 the President and the National Security Council reaffirmed the policy of setting stockpiling goals on the assumption that a war would last at least five years.

The policies followed by the government in the acquisition of materials for the stockpile did not apply to the sale of stockpiled items no longer needed because of changes in wartime requirements. The stockpiling legislation provides for the sale of excess materials from the stockpile only by order of the President, by order of the Office of Emergency Planning—the successor agency to the ODM—or by a resolution of Congress following a finding by the President that supplies of a material are no longer needed. Furthermore, there must be agreement among the Departments of Interior, Commerce, State, Agriculture, and Defense that the sale of materials would not be harmful to the interests of these departments or to the nation.

"The hearings demonstrated," said the Symington subcommittee report, "that attempts to dispose of materials from the national stockpile have thus far been rather ineffectual. There have been only two large-scale disposals, in rubber and tin. It is significant that there are no producers of natural rubber and tin in the United States and this could well account for the fact that the only two large disposals have been in these materials."

But even the sale of natural rubber did not come until several years after it was suggested that the rubber was no longer needed because of the development of synthetic rubber. John L. Collyer, a former president of the B. F. Goodrich Company and a spokesman for the manufacturers of rubber in the United States, suggested as early as 1951 that the government already had a surplus of rubber. It was not, however, until 1954 that the government stopped buying rubber to increase the size of the stockpile although some purchases continued until 1959 to replace stockpiled rubber that had deteriorated.

Until 1959, the subcommittee report noted, efforts to reduce the total size of the stockpile by selling the surplus rubber on hand were opposed by the State Department which, according to the report, "adamantly refused to agree to any rubber disposal plan because it was felt that such a disposal would seriously depreciate the world price of rubber, to the great disadvantage of such southeast Asian countries as Indonesia, Malaya, Burma, Siam, and others whose economies were largely tied to the production and export of natural rubber."

Yet even though a reduction in the size of the rubber stockpile began in 1959, by the end of 1961 the stockpile contained over a million long tons of rubber—one third more than was needed. Disposals of surplus stocks of stockpiled tin did not begin until 1961, and then not until after the government had carefully tested market reactions by offering to sell small amounts each week for twenty-eight weeks.

The names of prominent political leaders also figured in the testimony on stockpiling heard by the Symington subcommittee. The interest taken by political figures in the stockpile was another indication of the political pressures constantly being brought to bear on programs whose sole purpose was supposed to be to provide for the defense of the United States.

The best known political figure called to testify before the subcommittee was George M. Humphrey, who before becoming President Eisenhower's first Secretary of the Treasury in 1953 was chairman of the board of the M. A. Hanna Company of Cleveland, a huge mining concern. At issue in Humphrey's testimony was a contract for the production of nickel for the stockpile signed early in 1953 shortly before Humphrey took office as Secretary of the Treasury. Eisenhower had announced in the middle of November 1952 that Humphrey would be his Secretary of the Treasury.

The contract was negotiated because the United States depended almost entirely on foreign sources, principally in Canada, for its nickel. Testimony before the subcommittee by government officials indicated that the Hanna Company was able to drive a hard bargain with the government because of the desperate American need for nickel production. In a separate investigation of the contract, part of which involved the sale of a government nickel smelter to the Hanna company, the GAO found that Hanna got the smelter, which cost the government $22,800,000 to build, by paying only $1,700,000. The smelter was located near Riddle, Oregon, close to nickel deposits owned by Hanna. An auditor for the GAO told the Symington subcommittee that Hanna earned more than $15 million on sales of nickel to the government during the 1950's and that this represented a 57 percent profit on sales, 135 percent profit on costs, and 457 percent profit on its capital investment.

The Symington subcommittee concluded that "Hanna was interested in entering the refined nickel business on a permanent basis, not just in mining the nickel ore" and that "Hanna wanted a government contract with a guaranteed market, so it could, during the period of the contract, develop a commercial market against the time when shipments to the government would end" and, finally, that "Hanna contemplated the government would be selling much of Hanna's ferronickel production to industry, thereby stimulating a commercial demand for Hanna's product over the government contract period." Ferronickel is a nickel alloy used in the production of steel.

"It was therefore important to Hanna's long-range plans," the Symington subcommittee concluded in its report, "for the government to sell some of the Hanna ferronickel to industry. Accordingly, when Mr. Humphrey, as Secretary of the Treasury and a member of the Defense Mobilization Board, participated —which he testified he did—in decisions dealing with the sale and deferral of stockpile nickel to industry, in 1955, 1956, and 1957, he was assisting Hanna in its introduction of ferronickel to industry. . . . This assistance could only be of great value to the corporations in which he and his family still maintained a 14 percent interest." In his testimony before the subcommittee, Humphrey denied that the nickel contract resulted in unusually high profits for the Hanna company or that political influence figured in any of Hanna's dealings with the government.

Other political figures whose names came up during the Symington subcommittee hearings were Sinclair Weeks, President Eisenhower's Secretary of Commerce, who according to the subcommittee report sought special assistance along with Humphrey for a friend whose company had contracted to sell copper to the government for the stockpile; Thomas E. Dewey, the Republican presidential nominee in 1944 and 1948, whose law firm represented an aluminum supplier; and John Hay Whitney, the publisher of the New York *Herald Tribune,* who was also chairman of the board of the Freeport Sulphur Company and as such was interested in nickel contracts with the government.

In June 1956 the late Douglas McKay, who had resigned as Secretary of the Interior to seek a Senate seat from Oregon, wrote to Arthur S. Flemming, director of the Office of Defense Mobilization, to ask that he continue the purchase of chromite through a depot established in Oregon and that an announcement of this decision be made as soon as possible. A week later Flemming wired McKay: "In reply to your letter of June 18, in testimony today before the House Committee on Insular Affairs I will make the following statement relative to metallurgical chromite: 'The Department of the Interior has advised us that continuation of the program until the entire quota of 200,000 tons has been purchased may serve to develop a significant mobilization base. Therefore, I have authorized the General Services Administration to extend the program until June 30, 1959.'"

Not only were strategic and critical materials stockpiled during the 1950's in quantities far in excess of military requirements, the stockpiling continued on the basis of what were essentially World War II needs rather than on the basis of what would be needed in the event of nuclear war. Throughout the 1950's military strategy underwent significant changes and shifts dictated by the developments and realities of nuclear conflict; yet, the composition and purposes of the stockpile remained about the same as they had been at the end of a war of the kind that in all likelihood would never be fought again by the United States.

"It is now clear," concluded the Symington subcommittee in its report, "that, from the standpoint of our national security, much of the present stockpile is not needed. On the other hand, we are lacking in products essential to our survival. Therefore, the reconstitution of 'stockpiles' in consonance with modern strategic assumptions should be a matter of concern to the government and the American public."

The report noted that "there is a strong tendency to prepare for possible future hostilities with the weapons and tactics of the last war" and that "while, at its inception in 1946, the stockpile may have served a purpose, for almost a decade its very existence had produced a Maginot Line complex with respect to that part of the nation's resources allocated to the national defense."

The subcommittee foresaw four possible kinds of war that the United States should now be prepared to fight. One was a conventional war in which nuclear weapons of mass destruction would not be used. The second possibility was counter-insurgency operations involving action against subversive guerrilla units seeking to undermine local and national governments through raids, sabotage, and infiltration. The third possibility was defined by the subcommittee as limited sea war with attempts to attain a partial or complete blockade through the use of submarines. Finally, there was the possibility of general nuclear war with the likelihood of massive worldwide destruction.

"Of all these types of possible future struggle," said the subcommittee, "in only óne, limited conventional war, would a raw materials stockpile have real utility. Because of the possibility of escalation into nuclear exchange, however, even limited general conventional war might not be of long duration. Therefore, it is possible there will be little need for raw materials even based on current reduced three-year planning.

"A Korean-type action seems a possibility," the subcommittee went on to say in its report, "and counter-insurgency operations may become continuous by the end of the 1960's; but it would also seem possible for the economy to supply the needs for counter-insurgency and Korean-type operations without resort to stockpiled raw materials; our access to oversea supplies would not suffer serious interruption."

The subcommittee concluded that not only were excessive supplies of materials being stockpiled but also that the wrong kind of things were being hoarded.

"In case what we all hope will never occur does occur, namely, a nuclear war," the subcommittee said, "we believe considerable effort should also be expended to determine if stockpiles could be created which would effect a substantial saving of lives. Such stockpiles, however, would not be raw materials. The prime need would be for certain finished articles necessary to aid the population in the effort to survive. Therefore the present inventories of strategic and critical materials are in large measure unsuitable, if the need for them is measured against realistic strategic assumptions."

The subcommittee suggested that such things as processed foods, medical supplies, materials to provide sanitation needs, lumber, cement, asphalt, plumbing fixtures, pumps, steel beams, concrete reinforcing rods, and other construction materials should be stockpiled along with diesel oil, gasoline, lubricants, and other critical petroleum products to help the survivors of a nuclear attack try to reestablish at least a rudimentary civilization.

"We should bear in mind," the subcommittee concluded, "that the national stockpile was created to serve the national defense, not the total economy. . . . If an assessment of the future demonstrates that a substantial part of the stockpile is surplus, that hard fact must be faced. The economic impact of such a finding could be tempered by wise administration and close cooperation between government and affected industries. Fear of any economic impact, however, cannot be permitted to result in the continuance of a war plan much of which, in reality, has been obsolete since the first atomic explosion."

Although the subcommittee recommended the development of a program for the gradual disposal of stockpiled materials that are no longer needed, the value of the materials in the stockpile was still $8.5 billion in the fall of 1964, a year after the subcommittee published its report. In February 1962, when Kennedy called for an investigation of the stockpile, its value was estimated at $8.9 billion. Thus, in nearly three years, the value of materials in the stockpile declined by only $400 million.

The stockpile remains large because so many mining industries and other groups have a vested interest in it. Such large quantities of so many materials are stockpiled that any effort to dispose of some of the materials could have an adverse effect on their market price.

The story of the stockpile dramatically illustrates the difficulties inherent in efforts to reduce the government's role in a program that continues to benefit many segments of the economy, even though the program is no longer needed to fulfill the defense purposes for which it was originally developed.

CHAPTER

The Disarming Question

REPRESENTATIVE CRAIG HOSMER of California, a Republican member of the Joint Atomic Energy Committee, walked to the well of the House one day in November 1963 and solemnly warned his colleagues against "nutball . . . people" and "domestic idiots." He was referring to the 210 men and women working for the two-year-old United States Arms Control and Disarmament Agency. The Congressman was alarmed because the House was being asked to increase spending for arms control and disarmament studies from less than $7 million a year to $15 million.

"They are going to hire, in part at least," said Hosmer, "the type that come in and write papers for the Disarmament Agency and who will tell us that this nation must not have civil defense because it is provocative to the Russians. . . . That is how nutball these people are who are going to get part of this money that you folk are going to authorize today. . . . That is how silly it is. They will come in and try to lower the defense capability and safety of the people of this country. . . . I think it is time this country put its foot on—puts a lid on—this expenditure. A good job can be done with $7.5 million a year.

The agency should be working to protect the people of the United States not only from its foreign enemies but from its domestic idiots. Let us not give them money to spend foolishly or dangerously."

While Hosmer was concerned about "nutballs" and "domestic idiots," Democratic Representative Robert L. F. Sikes of Florida was worried about the Disarmament Agency's effects on domestic hunters.

"There have been indications," Sikes declared, "that the agency, failing to achieve concrete results on the international scene, or in its zeal to show United States support for general disarmament, could turn to domestic regulation of firearms in order to show reason for its continued existence. Assurances of officials of the Arms Control and Disarmament Agency have not dispelled this fear. After all, they can speak only for themselves—not for their successors. Therefore, magazines like *Guns & Ammo, Outdoor Life, Sports Afield,* and the *National Rifleman,* and that great organization of sportsmen, the National Rifle Association, with a host of sportsmen throughout the nation, want it made absolutely clear that the Arms Control and Disarmament Act does not include the elimination of private ownership of firearms as part of the proposed disarmament program."

And so the debate went as the afternoon wore on until Democratic Representative Leonard Farbstein of New York said, with considerable exasperation: "A most amazing thing has taken place this afternoon. That is the amount of excitement that has been engendered by an authorization bill seeking to increase the sum of money for arms control and disarmament. . . . I was present when the $50 billion was appropriated for arms and armaments and certainly there was not anywhere near this excitement. . . . We are just paring cherries."

Among the projects that the Disarmament Agency wanted to carry out with the additional funds were studies evaluating the impact of cutbacks in defense spending on employment and

134

other economic activity on a regional as well as on an industry-by-industry basis.

Not all of the members of Congress take such a vituperative view toward the tiny Disarmament Agency as does Hosmer or as suspicious a view as that expressed by Sikes, but in 1963 Congress did refuse the agency's request for more money. In the House this decision was made after a debate that was almost as long as the discussions earlier in the year on the $50 billion defense budget, which was approved by a unanimous vote.

The Arms Control and Disarmament Agency, set up by legislation in 1961 formalizing government disarmament work that began in the mid-1950's, has come under sharp attack in its short life despite its limited budget and even more limited activities.

"My mail," Republican Senator Thomas H. Kuchel of California told the Senate in October 1963, "indicates that thousands and thousands of Californians remain firmly wedded to the following fantastic fairy tales: that the Arms Control Agency can and will disarm the United States of America; that the law establishing the agency constitutes treason; that the United States proposes unilaterally to turn over its armed forces to the United Nations; that this act will place a Russian, the Under Secretary for Political and Security Council Affairs at the United Nations, in command of our forces and a world peace force."

The attacks on the Disarmament Agency became so outrageous in 1963 that even the American Legion, a supporter of the agency but hardly an enthusiast for unilateral disarmament, devoted a considerable portion of an issue of its monthly magazine to an article setting out the facts about the agency and pointing out that its functions are entirely advisory.

Most senators and representatives do not like to think about disarmament, let alone vote money for disarmament studies. In the fall of 1962 the staff of a subcommittee of the Senate

Foreign Relations Committee completed a survey of the problems defense contractors might have in converting to other work. The study, made for a group of senators headed by Hubert H. Humphrey of Minnesota, has never been made public. It has been kept secret because influential senators feared its publication would feed the Soviet propaganda line that the United States needs large expenditures for arms to keep its economy prosperous.

Many members of Congress act at times as if they were trying to prove that the Communist charges are true. During a 1963 discussion on the Senate floor of the advisability of awarding more defense contracts to depressed areas with chronic unemployment problems, Democratic Senator Philip Hart of Michigan said: "If anyone who reads the [*Congressional*] *Record* for the past hour should want to support the old bromide that the Communists preach about us—that we cannot afford disarmament, and we are the threat to the peace—he probably would find a useful chapter. This is the tragedy of it all."

Senator Humphrey had led off the discussion by presenting a report by a subcommittee of the Senate Small Business Committee calling for the awarding of more defense contracts to companies with plants in depressed areas. Humphrey deplored the fact that only 4 percent of all defense spending found its way into depressed areas. He also noted that "the use of defense funds, the manner in which these funds are allocated in terms of services, personnel, or the procurement of supplies and equipment is of vital importance to the economic well-being of the nation" and that "if the defense dollar is to continue to be as big as it is in the total economy, and if there are problems of unemployment and economic dislocation because of government policy, we should try to consider the use of the defense dollar to relieve some of the conditions created by government policy."

Another concern of Humphrey's while he was in the Senate was small business, which gets only about 17 percent of all defense contracts. Small businesses do, however, receive a larger share of the defense dollar through the extensive subcontracting that is part of the defense program, but there are no accurate figures available even on the total amount of defense business that is subcontracted.

Although Humphrey was unable to get the Foreign Relations Committee to let him make public his disarmament report, he was able to use most of the facts in it in a Senate speeech in October 1962. They concerned the amount of business done by the leading defense contractors and the concentration of arms contracts in the hands of a relatively few firms—facts which have been well documented since that date.

In discussing the disarmament report, Humphrey said that "planning now and conducting the appropriate studies could make a major difference in keeping our economy at a high level during a transition period in which defense spending was decreasing and other levels of economic activity were increasing.... If we discuss the economic impact of disarmament on our economy, we shall reach the conclusion that not only is it possible to make such a conversion without serious dislocation, but it is also possible to have a vastly improved economy, one in which economic expansion moves rapidly and in which the production of goods and services increases for the common good."

Disarmament may still be a long way off; but during the three years since the Senate subcommittee study of the economic consequences of disarmament, there have been signs, chiefly the test-ban treaty, that the Soviet Union may be weary of the arms race. In the United States it has become evident that the nuclear weapons stockpile cannot be increased forever. President Johnson's decision to reduce defense spending in 1964 by cutting back government purchases of fissionable materials was a belated recognition of the nation's overkill capacity. Writing in the April 1964 issue of *Foreign Affairs* shortly after he left the government, former Deputy Secretary of Defense Roswell

L. Gilpatric noted that "we are past the peak of the very large expenses involved in building up our Polaris and Minuteman missile forces," that we are "approaching the point at which further increases in strategic delivery vehicles promise little meaningful military advantage," and that defense spending probably could be reduced 25 percent by 1970.

Still, there is great reluctance both on Capitol Hill and within the Johnson Administration to develop plans for converting defense-production facilities to other uses and for helping defense workers find new jobs. But despite the understandable fears of Soviet intentions, the very magnitude of our involvement in the defense effort is beginning to inspire counteracting fears for the stability of the American economy and is spurring, rather than hampering, the planning of measures to offset disarmament, when and if it comes.

Despite all the opposition it has encountered on Capitol Hill, the Arms Control and Disarmament Agency has produced the best study of the way in which defense spending might decline and the problems a cutback in armaments might bring to the United States economy.

The agency's study was made by a nine-member panel headed by economist Emile Benoit of Columbia University and published in 1962 by the agency in a twenty-eight page pamphlet entitled "Economic Impacts of Disarmament." A somewhat expanded version of the study, called "The Economic and Social Consequences of Disarmament," was also published in 1962 and submitted by the United States to the United Nations as part of an international examination of domestic disarmament problems conducted by the United Nations.

The panel estimated that if world conditions made disarmament possible, United States defense spending would decline over a period of twelve years from its present level of about $50 billion to $10 billion. The panel's report divided the twelve years into three periods. During the first three years, it was estimated that defense spending would be cut back $17 billion followed by a second three-year stage of a further reduction of $12 billion. During the final six years of this phased-out program of arms reduction, the panel projected further cutbacks totaling $13.5 billion.

Although United States defense expenditures would amount to only $10 billion at the end of this twelve-year period, the panel estimated that the United States would take on $7 billion in new expenditures to help finance an international organization that unquestionably would be needed for inspection, police, and deterrent functions. So the net impact of the panel's assumptions would mean total defense and international arms control inspection costs at the end of twelve years of $17 billion, about one third the present defense budget.

The panel went on to note that in addition to America's costs involved in international policing and inspection operations, increases in expenditures for the government's space and civilian atomic energy programs might together amount to $2.5 billion annually during the early years of a disarmament program and thus provide some cushion for the decline in spending for armaments. These projections did not involve additional space programs that might be adopted specifically to offset disarmament cutbacks.

And what would the effect of such reductions in defense spending be on the nation's economy? The panel pointed out that a net reduction of $5 billion a year in the defense budget would amount to less than 1 percent of the gross national product and thus would have a considerably smaller impact than when World War II ended and the reduction in arms spending totaled 30 percent of the GNP, or when the Korean hostilities ended with defense cutbacks amounting to 3 percent of the GNP.

But the successful transition of the economy at the end of World War II from war to peace is irrelevant to the present discussions of what might follow in the wake of an East-West disarmament agreement. During World War II automobiles and other consumer goods were not produced. So by the time the war was over, a large demand for consumer goods had built up. Savings were at a record high, and consumers were ready to cut loose.

Today shelves and showrooms are bulging with goods, and many factories are idle part of the year because of lagging demand. The large part of the economy devoted to the production and sale of consumer goods hardly needs either the factory space or the manpower that would be released by a cutback in defense spending. Furthermore, many of the largest producers of armaments and other defense materials have never had to deal with a civilian market—or last dealt with one in the long-ago days before World War II.

The experience following the end of the Korean War, which is relevant, hardly augers well for the future. The $2 billion reduction of nondefense expenditures that accompanied the sharp cutbacks in defense spending in 1954 contributed to the general slowdown in economic activity during the late 1950's. In that period, too, defense spending soon was on the increase again, and by the end of the 1950's the defense budget was even larger than it had been during the Korean War.

The Disarmament Agency panel concluded that any Administration would hardly stand by while the defense budget was substantially cut back, that "public pressures would be strong to reduce taxes and to permit the expansion of some high priority nondefense government programs that are being kept on ice during the period of heavy defense budgets," and that "perhaps the chief danger of a precipitant decline would be psychological.

"We would be facing an extended series of future defense cuts over more than a decade ahead," the panel's report continued. "We have never had a situation exactly parallel to this in our history, and we cannot be sure just how this would affect business and consumer anticipations and expenditure plans. . . .

"A great deal might depend," the report added, "on whether the government could provide sufficient reassurance by demonstrating that a definite program of offsets had been readied and would be promptly implemented. In this connection, people's expectations would be considerably affected by their experience in the years prior to disarmament. If public policy had succeeded in reducing excessive unemployment and restoring a rapid rate of growth, the economy could more readily absorb deflationary impacts without serious hurt, and confidence in the government's power to protect prosperity would be higher. On the whole, it is our judgment that a sharp letdown during disarmament remains unlikely and should be avoidable if the government exercises a modicum of economic sense, foresight, and courageous leadership."

One of the problems resulting from disarmament, the panel said, would probably be the strong public demand that savings accruing from cutbacks in defense spending be applied to reducing the public debt. Public opinion surveys have shown that the use of such savings for a reduction in the public debt is as popular as a cut in taxes. Public opinion polls taken in 1964 also found no great demand among voters for a large expansion of nondefense spending.

Yet, as the panel pointed out, a reduction in federal expenditures when matched with a decline in taxes "will not provide quite as much of a stimulus to the economy as is lost by the decline in public expenditure," largely because not all of the increased disposable income in the hands of consumers will be immediately translated into expenditures.

"A second kind of difficulty that might arise if the offsets to defense cuts were mainly in the form of tax cuts," the panel commented, "is related to the possible disadvantages of functioning with a permanently smaller public sector in the economy, at least smaller relatively to total GNP. It is generally agreed that the greatly enlarged public sector since World War II, resulting from heavy defense expenditures, has provided additional protection against depressions, since this sector is not responsive to contraction in the private sector and provides a sort of buffer or balance wheel in the economy. The high tax rate required by this high level of government expenditures provides a large volume of revenue which is very sensitive to changes in income, so that shocks to the economy are in good part absorbed in declines in taxes rather than in disposable income. A reduction in the size of the public sector would weaken this type of protection."

Again and again, the panel emphasized the need for the government to plan well in advance the detailed measures to be undertaken to offset the necessary adjustments in the wake of disarmament to "permit us to take advantage of the great opportunities which disarmament will afford for the improved allocation of our resources and to help prevent our readjustment measures being too much influenced by considerations of expediency and by short-run political pressures." The panel spoke particularly of the need for government programs in the fields of education and research, transportation, urban renewal, and public health.

"The balance struck between tax reduction and increased government spending," said the panel, "will be governed by the relative importance accorded to private demand for such goods and services as food, clothing, housing, recreation, health, higher education, machine tools, research, and development—as against public demand for school construction, teacher training, roads, space exploration, urban renewal, area redevelopment, public health and social services. . . . Policy will also have to strike the appropriate balance between those measures that satisfy present wants and those that promote the long-term dynamic growth of the economy."

The panel noted that the biggest readjustment problems would of course come in the industries where there is the greatest concentration of defense contracts—ordnance, aircraft, shipbuilding, electronics—and in the states where defense spending is concentrated—California, Washington, Texas, Kansas, Utah.

To help these people and these industries, directly, the panel would have the government increase unemployment compensation, greatly expand manpower retraining programs, help pay the moving costs of workers who must go to other cities to get work, encourage higher severance pay by making it a legitimate cost of defense contracts, and help companies plan the conversion of their facilities from defense work to the manufacture of products for the civilian economy.

The panel's eight conclusions sum up the problems and prospects:

(1) That disarmament of the type and at the pace which the panel considers to be implied by the United States Program for General and Complete Disarmament in a Peaceful World (submitted to the United Nations on September 25, 1961), after allowance for proposed expansion in National Aeronautics and Space Administration (NASA) and civilian Atomic Energy Commission (AEC) programs and the requirements of disarmament inspection and international peace enforcement, should create small danger of provoking immediate depression in our economy, assuming sensible adjustment policies and vigorous government leadership to dispel adverse effects on business and consumer anticipations and to provide reassurance that aggregate demand will not be allowed to decline precipitantly;

(2) That a steady decline in defense spending spread over several years may prove a significant drag on the economy and pose serious problems for policymakers. These problems can be mastered by the application of appropriate policies, the chief obstacles to which would be political resistance rather than deficiencies in our economic knowledge;

(3) That structural problems in particular industries or areas are unavoidable and could be serious for the individuals, companies, and communities prominently affected;

(4) That the alleviation of these structural difficulties may

143

require a variety of adjustment programs, some providing assistance for retraining, temporary support, and relocation of individuals and reconversion and diversification of enterprises; some promoting the importation of new industries into areas hard hit by the closing of defense plants and installations; and some, perhaps, seeking new publicly supported uses of national importance for part of our existing defense resources, particularly our capabilities in research and development;

(5) That included in the latter category might be research and development programs on technological bottlenecks impeding international economic development, which could also make a significant contribution to one of our major foreign policy objectives;

(6) That the impact of disarmament would only accentuate structural problems which already exist and which will have to be solved anyhow if the nation is to produce up to its full potentialities;

(7) That if these problems are overcome, achievement of major national goals will be greatly facilitated by the use of the human and material resources released from the defense program;

(8) That within wide limits the nation can afford to have as high or as low a level of defense expenditures as is deemed politically desirable and should feel no constraint on the economic side in adjusting defense expenditures to whatever level seems best to accord with our political objectives. However, advance planning by government at all levels and by business firms, labor unions, and other private organizations is required if the economy is to adjust smoothly to significant changes in the level of defense spending, particularly such as would result from general and complete disarmament.

The members of the Disarmament Agency panel, all but four of whom were government economists, were concerned over the political problems involved in convincing Congress that a substantial reduction in defense spending should not be reflected only in tax cuts but that much of the money should be transferred from the Pentagon's account to meet the needs of education, transportation, crowded cities, and depressed areas.

Their concern is understandable in view of the experience since 1961 with the redevelopment program, which tries to help bring industry to depressed areas, and with the manpower-retraining legislation. To get the depressed-areas program through Congress President Kennedy had to agree to turn it into a pork barrel. So many rural areas were made eligible for these loans, to get support for the program from Southern members of Congress, that the Area Redevelopment Administration has been unable to concentrate its efforts in the depressed communities that need help the most.

The manpower-retraining program has suffered from congressional suspicions of federal expenditures designed to help solve America's social problems. Congress has provided little money to train the unskilled because such programs quickly become entangled in racial prejudices as well as fears of an increased federal role in education.

It was for these practical political reasons, Senator Douglas once said, that most of the liberal Democrats in Congress had abandoned their efforts to increase government spending to provide for the needs of Americans and had enthusiastically embraced tax reduction as the way to a better life. The tax-reduction route had once been sound conservative Republican doctrine scorned by liberal Democrats. Douglas said that he and other liberals had reluctantly concluded that Congress would not vote the funds needed for adequate social-welfare programs, so why not try to stimulate the economy by cutting taxes?

Persuasive and level-headed as the argument put forth by the Disarmament Agency panel was, it stirred few Americans until in the summer of 1963, a year and a half after its publication, the United States and the Soviet Union agreed to stop tests of nuclear weapons except for those that could be performed underground.

One of the few persons who remained concerned about the economic consequences of disarmament during this eighteen-month period was Seymour Melman, professor of industrial and management engineering at Columbia University. Although Melman is best known for his vigorous advocacy of the idea of "overkill," by which he means the accumulation of a stockpile of nuclear weapons far in excess of any potential need, he also has been a persistent advocate of planning to offset the domestic economic effects of disarmament.

"Military spending has caused economic stagnation," Melman argued in the 1963 pamphlet "A Strategy for American Security," which he edited. "Two thirds of America's prime productive resources—her engineers and scientists—are now engaged in military rather than civilian production. The manufacture of military goods, however intricate, results in no further production."

Not only did Melman maintain that the United States already has a far greater number of nuclear weapons than would ever be needed to repulse a Soviet attack, but he and six other professors who collaborated with him in the writing of the pamphlet outlined how defense spending could be reduced to little more than $9 billion a year. They would use at least half of the resulting saving of $40 billion or more a year to finance such public expenditures as education, urban renewal, urban transit, public health, the control of water, air, soil, and other resources, and increased economic aid to foreign countries. A large tax cut to stimulate private spending is also part of the Melman program.

Although Melman's "overkill" thesis has been subjected to considerable attack from the Air Force and its friends, Melman has been responsible for increasing public interest in both the problems of excessive military expenditures and the need for making plans for disarmament or for the time when the armed services may actually have enough weapons.

In 1964 Melman released the results of a survey which showed that a total of 67,000 technical, clerical, and production employees were being laid off by nineteen major defense contractors because of a cutback in arms needs.

"These layoffs in highly skilled occupations underscore the special problems of converting from military to civilian work," Melman said. "Military-oriented skills are often not readily applicable to civilian work. That is why there is unemployment in these occupations and regions in the midst of an upswing in general employment.

"Why do these layoffs occur?" Melman asked in a statement he released along with his survey. "In the words of the marketing manager of a leading electronics firm: 'The distant early warning system [DEW line] was built and will not be built over again. Therefore, our firm must lay off the research, development, design, and production employees who did this work.'

"Even where production of major weapons is continuing," Melman added, "designs have tended to be standardized, mainly because little is to be gained from large investments in tiny improvements. An intercontinental missile that travels two minutes faster and lands a calculated twenty-five yards closer is not meaningfully altered, though the cost of these technical changes would be very great."

Melman also noted that Representative Vinson said early in 1964 that "we are reaching a point in several areas, principally missiles, where we are coming up pretty close to our total needs. And we simply do not need to buy as many of the items as we did before. As a matter of fact, we are stronger in our defense today than we have ever been in any peacetime period before."

Senator McGovern first suggested the establishment of a National Economic Conversion Commission in a Senate speech in the summer of 1963. This was the speech in which he declared that the United States had far more nuclear weapons than it would ever need. In October 1963, McGovern formally introduced his conversion legislation, saying:

"Our military security requires that our defense planners be permitted a considerable degree of flexibility in weapons production and modification. As matters now stand, necessary changes or reductions in weapons systems or defense installations are often vigorously resisted by the affected communities and their political spokesmen. Such political and economic pressures which freeze unneeded plants or installations into the defense establishment weaken our overall strength. . . . But . . . in the absence of alternative plans, who can blame a community, or a labor leader, or a congressman, for vigorous opposition to the loss of a valuable payroll or dividend?

"A second reason for planning conversion is that we have an obligation to protect our citizens in the armed forces and defense industries against an economic calamity. We need to replace uncertainty and anxiety with the assurance that conversion to civilian production can actually be a hopeful opportunity for the American people. . . . In turn, the development of competence for conversion will make possible more realistic appraisals of defense spending, for then decisions on the termination of contracts or the closing of installations to meet legitimate efficiency and security requirements need not be blunted by concern for economic dislocation. This is bound to improve both the short- and long-term design and administration of our security policies. It will also add new force to disarmament discussions by removing fear of the economic consequences. . . .

"These proposed steps can help give our people a solid basis for confidence in their own and our nation's future. With other related efforts, they can demonstrate that the best path to American prosperity and economic growth lies not in a constantly expanding arms race but in carefully gauged steps toward peace."

McGovern's Economic Conversion Commission would be set up within the Executive Office of the President, would be headed by the Secretary of Commerce, and would have as members the Secretaries of Defense, Agriculture, Labor, and Interior, the Chairmen of the Atomic Energy Commission and the Council of Economic Advisers, and the Directors of the Arms Control and Disarmament Agency and the National Aeronautics and Space Administration.

Under McGovern's proposal, the commission would be responsible for drafting a blueprint setting out appropriate actions that should be taken by the departments and agencies of the federal government to facilitate the conversion of arms plants to peacetime production. This blueprint, said McGovern, should include the preparation of schedules of possible private and public investment patterns resulting from different degrees of economic conversion as well as studies of the possible effects on employment of such conversion. McGovern would require that these reports be submitted by the commission to Congress within a year after the enactment of his legislation.

During its first year the commission would also organize what McGovern called a National Conference on Industrial Conversion and Growth to focus attention on the problems of conversion and to stimulate discussion and study of the problems throughout the economy. The bill also provides for the commission to work with the governors of all the states to encourage, in McGovern's words, "appropriate and timely preparation in support of conversion capability."

Other sections of the bill would require companies that have had defense contracts for at least a year covering 25 percent or more of their employees to set up their own conversion planning committees.

In arguing for his legislation, McGovern told the Senate that "our present level of military spending, far from strengthening the economy, is actually distorting and restricting the economy, weakening the competitive position of our civilian industries in both domestic and international trade, and seriously aggravating our balance-of-payments problem."

He went on to say that "a costly nuclear warhead resting in the arsenal has little or no impact on the economy, whereas a similar investment in updated machine tools or classrooms or scholarships pays compound dividends" and that "few Americans realize that the gleaming new civilian plants of West Germany, Japan and Italy—the hapless Axis powers of eighteen years ago—have left the United States with the distinction of operating the most outdated metal-working machinery of any major industrial country."

McGovern has also noted that, in marked contrast to the lack of conversion planning in the 1960's, during World War II planning for a return to a peacetime economy started as early as 1943 under the direction of the Committee for Economic Development, a private planning group that is still in existence. The Senator has pointed out, too, that planning by private industry to convert its facilities to peacetime production after World War II was "mightily assisted" by such federal programs as the GI Bill of Rights and favorable tax credits and monetary policies. "This planning," McGovern commented, "paid off in the smooth transition to a civilian economy we experienced after World War II. Proper planning today will yield similar dividends."

Proposals similar to McGovern's were put forward earlier by three other senators. But, to remove the plans from the supercharged atmosphere of disarmament discussions, all three broadened their plans to include the equally difficult problems caused by automation and other changes in technology.

Senator Humphrey advocated the establishment of a Commission on Automation, Technology, and Employment which would direct particular attention to the economic consequences of disarmament. Senator Hart proposed a Commission on the Application of Technology to Community and Manpower Needs, one of the benefits of which would have been, in the Senator's cautious words, "a greater understanding of the feasibility of a transfer of industrial skills and technology from defense-oriented programs to work on programs in the civilian sector." Senator Clark not only sponsored a Planning for Peace Resolution, he even held hearings in the fall of 1963 on some of the employment problems that might result from disarmament. The hearings produced valuable testimony and studies on the economic consequences of disarmament as well as on other problems stemming from changes in industrial development and in technology.

All of these proposals were somewhat blunted in December 1963 when President Johnson set up a ten-member Committee on the Economic Impact of Defense and Disarmament. The establishment of the committee followed strident protests by members of Congress against the closing of twenty-six military bases ordered, with the President's approval, by Secretary McNamara in December 1963.

In a memorandum outlining the purposes of the committee, Johnson noted that in June 1963 Walter W. Heller, who was then Chairman of the President's Council of Economic Advisers, had organized an informal group to review and coordinate the work of federal agencies relating to the economic impact of defense and disarmament. The new committee, said the President, would continue this work on a more formal and permanent basis.

The President gave the committee responsibility for "the review and coordination of activities in the various departments and agencies designed to improve our understanding of the economic impact of defense expenditures and of changes either in the composition or the total level of such expenditures."

But Johnson severely restricted the activities of the committee when he said in the same memorandum that he did not expect it "to undertake studies of its own, but rather to evaluate and to coordinate these existing efforts, and if it seems desirable, to recommend additional studies."

The President's committee has turned out to be a bland and disappointing version of what McGovern, Humphrey, Hart, and Clark had in mind. They had been calling for action as well as study. Some members of Congress who are concerned about disarmament problems suspected that Johnson hurriedly established the committee largely to sidetrack the more meaningful proposals for study and action that had been made on Capitol Hill. The President was reported at the time of the establishment of the committee to have been particularly concerned about Senator Clark's plans for further hearings on the economic consequences of disarmament—hearings which might have led to increasing congressional demands for action on these enormous problems. Such demands could have proved to be embarrassing to Johnson in the 1964 election year.

It was not in fact until March 1964 that Johnson got around to formally naming Gardner Ackley, now chairman of his Council of Economic Advisers, as chairman of the committee, too. The other nine members, also appointed in March 1964, represented the Defense, Labor and Commerce Departments, the Atomic Energy Commission, the Arms Control and Disarmament Agency, the National Aeronautics and Space Administration, the Bureau of the Budget, the Office of Emergency Planning, and the Office of Science and Techology.

In May 1964 Senator McGovern complained that the committee had met only a few times and that "in the five months since the President's memorandum it has not even completed its organizational work, much less begun the assigned task of coordinating government activity in the conversion field."

McGovern said that he had asked the committee to study the impact of the closing of the Black Hills Army Depot in his state of South Dakota, a shutdown that was ordered by Secretary McNamara in the spring of 1964, but he was informed that the committee had no staff members available for such a study. McGovern also said that other members of Congress had received the same sort of replies when they had made similar requests of the committee.

McGovern went on to note the inadequacies of the two other federal agencies concerned with the economic impact of changes and cutbacks in the defense program. One, he pointed out, is the three-man Office of Economic Adjustment, which McNamara set up in the Defense Department in 1961 to help communities where defense installations are closed or curtailed or where defense contracts are canceled. The other operation is in the Disarmament Agency where a staff of four men is carrying on research into the economic impact of disarmament under the supervision of Archibald Alexander, a former Under Secretary of the Army, who is now assistant director of the Disarmament Agency. Finally, McGovern noted that the Atomic Energy Commission had just announced the establishment of a small office to help industry adjust to cutbacks in the production of nuclear materials.

When the Senate Commerce Committee finally got around to holding hearings on McGovern's economic conversion bill, the three witnesses who appeared to present the Johnson Administration's views on the legislation were extremely cool toward it. The Administration witnesses were Alexander, Ackley, and Cyrus Vance, who succeeded Roswell Gilpatric as Deputy Secretary of Defense in 1964.

"We are in complete agreement with the objectives of this bill," Vance said in summing up the Administration's position. "Although we consider that the legislation, under the present circumstances, is probably not necessary, we certainly have no objection to it or to other evidence of congressional interest in and approval of the efforts of the President's Committee on the Economic Impact of Defense and Disarmament."

Vance expressed particular opposition to the section of the McGovern bill requiring defense contractors to set up conversion committees. Vance argued that a Defense Department procurement regulation approved in the spring of 1964 permitted such conversion planning to be taken as an allowable cost on a defense contract and that therefore the provision in the McGovern legislation was not necessary. (McGovern eliminated this section in the 1965 version of his bill.)

In his own testimony before the Commerce Committee, McGovern maintained that many defense contractors would not engage in any planning unless the government required them to do so. "No question of government interference is presented here," McGovern added, "because these contractors are largely or entirely dependent upon government funds. This requirement would be no different in principle from the many other conditions a defense contractor must meet in order to be awarded a contract."

Despite the Administration's opposition to the McGovern bill, it had picked up 30 sponsors in the Senate by early 1965. The number of sponsors clearly indicated the increasing interest on Capitol Hill in the possible economic consequences of cutbacks in defense spending. Nevertheless, the legislation did not get beyond the hearing stage in 1964.

A further indication of the interest on Capitol Hill in defense conversion problems came in the summer of 1964 when both the Senate and the House approved with no opposition the establishment of a fourteen-member National Commission on Technology, Automation and Economic Progress which President Johnson had requested in his State of the Union message earlier in the year. The discussion of the legislation in both houses made it clear that although the commission's task would be much broader than that envisaged by Senator McGovern for his Conversion Commission, the economic consequences of disarmament would constitute an important part of the new commission's studies and findings.

In announcing his support for the commission, Senator Nelson said that it should "recommend ways to facilitate the carry-over of technological advances made in the defense industries into nonmilitary industries, so that consumers can share the benefits of scientific discoveries" and that the commission should also "assist companies which depend heavily on defense contracts in spreading out into other areas, so that the dependence of our nation's economy on military spending can be lessened."

Governors and legislators in such states as California and Washington that are heavily dependent on defense spending are acutely aware that disarmament could mean disaster for them unless adequate plans are made to cushion the impact of a sharp cutback in the purchase of arms and armaments. Governor Edmund G. Brown and other California political leaders have urged Congress to provide for more retraining programs as well as workers' moving allowances. Brown also would have the federal government provide grants to help defense-oriented communities plan for reconversion and to finance remodeling and retooling that might be needed to turn defense plants into modern factories for the production of consumer goods.

In 1963 Robert E. Rose, then director of Washington State's Department of Commerce and Economic Development, urged at a meeting of state planning agencies, support for a conference of officials of state governments to develop "some constructive steps toward the closer working liaison needed in this important area of planning and programming for disarmament." Rose noted that the states would most certainly be involved in the administration of such federal aid programs to ease readjustment problems as low-cost industrial loans, research and development funds for broad purposes, large-scale manpower retraining programs, and industrial relocation loans.

States like California and Washington also want the Defense Department to accelerate the promised development of methods for accurately forecasting defense spending over a five-year period. Such forecasts would be the essence of a much-discussed "Early Warning System" to alert companies and cities of changes in defense needs. But first the Defense Department must find out exactly where all of its contract dollars go. Through its own research agency, the Institute for Defense Analysis, it has, however, begun to make a comprehensive study not only to determine the impact defense spending has on communities but also to discover to what areas defense dollars flow through subcontracts.

Still, there remains a reluctance both on Capitol Hill and within the Johnson Administration to face head-on the question of the economic consequences of disarmament. Within the Administration the few measures that have been taken to study the problems of conversion and to help communities caught up in defense spending cutbacks have been half-hearted and far from adequate. In Congress no real pressure has yet developed behind proposals like Senator McGovern's for a conversion commission. Too many senators and representatives seem to want to believe that conversion problems will someday quietly disappear. Members of Congress also know that there are more votes in defense contracts than in disarmament plans.

"Cold war by its nature carries the implication of going on indefinitely," commented the *Morgan Guaranty Survey* in the summer of 1963. "Arms cutbacks, to most people, still mean only the massive, idealistic kind of disarmament that is a remote dream in today's world of tension. Accordingly, the real challenge of working out of the armaments bind is largely ignored. A few theoreticians tinker with models of an economy in which defense expenditures have been cut by half or more, but very little serious consideration is given to the problems of living with a gradual, modest step-down of the total."

As conservative a publication as the *Morgan Guaranty Survey* recognized the real problems of disarmament that government administrators and politicians would rather ignore. The *Morgan Guaranty Survey* advocated the granting of "a modest allowance" to defense contractors to help them conduct research into ways in which they could convert their facilities to peacetime production.

"Without provision of this type," said the *Survey,* "many defense companies—especially the smaller ones and those entirely or almost entirely engaged in military work—cannot afford to divert resources to disarmament insurance."

Through Secretary McNamara's leadership the Defense Department has demonstrated that programs that are no longer needed can be ended and that companies and communities can be helped to make the transition from defense to civilian work with a minimum of hardship to all concerned.

But the transition has been made successfully in the last few years for the most part in relatively small operations; and even in these cases, successful changeovers often have been carried out only because other government programs, projects, and contracts have been brought into the affected areas to provide new jobs.

CHAPTER 8

When the Bases Close

IN MARCH 1961, President Kennedy announced that fifty military bases would be closed. He did not immediately list the installations to be shut down but he did say they would include a Snark missile base. That was all the people in the town of Presque Isle in the potato country of Aroostook County, Maine, needed to know because they had the world's only Snark base. The Snark was an air-breathing missile that had become obsolete with the rapid development of more sophisticated weapons.

Although the installation had served as a missile base for only two years, the Air Force had contributed to the well-being of the Presque Isle economy for more than twenty years. Before being turned into a Snark base, the Presque Isle air field, located in the uppermost northeastern corner of the United States, had been the jumping off point for all trans-atlantic military flights and then, as airplanes were improved, a base for fighter-interceptor craft.

Airplanes, missiles, and potatoes had added up to prosperity for the people of Presque Isle, and the Air Force had brought more jobs and money to the community than had the potato business. Presque Isle is a city of only 13,000, and the Air Force had been providing 1,527 jobs—1,259 in the military and 268 for civilians—with an annual payroll of $3.5 million. In addition, the Air Force had been spending $1.8 million each year for food and other supplies in the area, and the federal government had been contributing $102,000 to the community's school system because of the extra burdens placed on it by the large number of children of military personnel, most of whom did not pay state or local taxes.

"The people of Presque Isle could have panicked; they could have wrung their hands in despair," Democratic Senator Edmund S. Muskie of Maine said two years after the announcement that the base would be closed. "They did neither. Calmly and intelligently, they considered the alternatives, sought all possible assistance, and embarked upon a program designed to achieve a practical solution to their problem."

Presque Isle had the good fortune to be one of the first communities to get assistance from the Office of Economic Adjustment in the Defense Department. The Office was established in May 1961 as a direct result of the base closings announced by Kennedy two months earlier.

That same month Senator Muskie headed a group of officials that met in Presque Isle to try to find solutions for the many problems that the base's closing would cause. By then, October 1, 1961 had been set as the date for closing the base. At the meeting were officials from the Defense, Commerce, and Agriculture Departments, all of whom outlined the kinds of federal programs and assistance available to the people of Presque Isle.

Following the meeting of businessmen and other leaders of the community with the federal officials, the Presque Isle City Council and the city's Chamber of Commerce held many other meetings to determine what the community should do to try to save itself from the economic consequences of the base's loss. Finally in July 1961, the community leaders formed the Presque

Isle Industrial Council to try to find new uses for the base, which had buildings spread over 2,100 acres, 17 acres of streets and parking spaces alone, sewer and water systems larger than those serving the city of Presque Isle itself, 144 fire hydrants, and miles of electrical systems, fences, sidewalks, and railroad track.

Lending a hand to these efforts was Robert Steadman, a political scientist and management expert who was hired by Secretary McNamara as the first director of the Department's Office of Economic Adjustment. With a small staff and little money at his disposal, however, Steadman was limited largely to cutting away red tape and breaking bottlenecks so that Presque Isle could obtain title as quickly as possible to the surplus air base buildings. The Office of Economic Adjustment can only direct communities to existing federal aid programs; it has no money to provide any direct help of its own. (In 1963 Steadman retired and was succeeded as head of the office by one of his assistants, Donald F. Bradford.)

By September 1961, the Presque Isle Industrial Council had hired a director and a staff and had decided to use money from local taxes to finance its program. On the council's seven-man board of directors were a doctor, a lawyer, an executive of a small manufacturing company, two executives from the electric utility in the area, a manager of a chain store, and an automobile dealer.

It did not take the Industrial Council long to move into action. A vocational training school had long been needed in this part of Maine, and with the aid of a $250,000 appropriation from the state legislature, the council was able to locate the Northwestern Maine Vocational Institute on part of the site of the air base. Eighty acres and fifty buildings valued at $3 million were given to the state by the federal government under provisions of laws providing for the donation of surplus lands and buildings to be used for educational purposes. Another $150,000 worth of surplus equipment at the air base was donated to the new school by the federal government. In 1964, in its second year of operation, the school had 150 students and by 1970 the enrollment is expected to reach seven hundred.

The vocational school soon got a neighbor on the air base site. The local school district needed land for a new junior high school, and it got twenty-six acres of the Air Force base. The Skyway Junior High School now occupies a modern building there with classroom space for six hundred pupils.

Presque Isle also needed a modern municipal airport. Through the Federal Aviation Agency and another program for the disposal of surplus lands and buildings, the city obtained without cost three large airplane hangars, a building that served as the missile-control headquarters, the old motor pool headquarters, and several warehouses. All of the buildings are now used by the Presque Isle Municipal Airport.

Still to be disposed of by the government were six large missile hangars, three large warehouses, six smaller warehouses, and other miscellaneous buildings. They were carefully appraised, and late in 1961 the government's General Services Administration said these properties were worth $56,000 and were available at that price to the Presque Isle Industrial Council. Despite misgivings of its own and cries of "white elephant!" from its critics, the council bought the remaining land and buildings.

It took less than a year, however, to prove that the decision was a wise one. Presque Isle's big break came in May 1962 when the Indian Head Plywood Company of Bethel, Vermont, signed a long-term lease for four of the large missile buildings and announced plans to employ five hundred persons to produce plywood and other wood products. When in full production the plant would need 10 million board feet of hardwood logs annually, and this would mean employment in the woods of Aroostook County for another four hundred to five hundred men.

An old airplane hangar was taken over by the International

161

Paper Company, which employed only fifteen persons at the start of its Presque Isle operations but planned to expand its payroll to 125 when the plant was in full production.

Other companies took over some of the remaining buildings and are using them as warehouses. These included H. P. Hood & Sons, Eastern States Farmers' Exchange, Presque Isle Starch Company, Northern Maine Aviation, Aroostook Shoe Company, American Propane Corporation, and Consolidated Printing Services. Altogether nineteen companies took space in buildings that were formerly a part of the Snark base and were taken over by the city of Presque Isle through its Industrial Council and leased by it to the firms. They form Presque Isle's thriving Skyway Industrial Park.

In addition, space has been found on the old air base site for research on potato storage problems being carried out by the University of Maine, a garage for the city highway department, an American Legion post, an indoor skating and hockey rink, and two curling rinks. Eighty acres of the base were developed as camping areas for Boy Scouts and Girl Scouts, and the base's picnic grounds were turned into a lake with camping facilities, trout fishing in a brook that flows into the lake, and even a seaplane base.

"When the city and chamber of commerce officials first undertook the task of buying and managing the base there were many people in Presque Isle who felt it would be the greatest 'white elephant' ever," James K. Keefe, executive director of the Presque Isle Industrial Council, said in 1963. "Today, everyone feels the closing of Presque Isle Air Force Base and the opening of Skyway Industrial Park, as it is now known, was about the best thing ever to happen to this city."

Presque Isle, which lost more than one thousand five hundred jobs when the Snark base closed down, gained two thousand jobs as a result of the development of the old Air Force facilities into an industrial park. The Presque Isle story was indeed a success story. It represented a successful transition from a highly military-oriented economy to an economy solidly based on the production of civilian goods.

The Defense Department's Office of Economic Adjustment showed the people of Presque Isle how the government could help them, principally through the donation of surplus lands and buildings but also with federal grants and loans if they were needed. But the Presque Isle success story was written largely by the businessmen and other leaders of the community who decided to take a chance on their ability to attract industry to the facilities that once served the base.

Another community that succeeded in overcoming a substantial cutback in defense spending was Wichita, Kansas, where the Boeing aircraft payroll which totaled thirty-five thousand in the late 1950's fell to eighteen thousand by 1962 following the completion of the production of B-52 planes. After the final decision to halt production of B-52's, announced in 1961 but not effective until the fall of 1962, representatives of the Office of Economic Adjustment met with Wichita businessmen and other civic leaders. Out of the meeting came a plan for a comprehensive evaluation of the city's advantages and disadvantages. The primary recommendation of the survey was for greater diversification of the city's economic base, which had been heavily dependent on the production of military aircraft.

As part of the diversification effort, the Defense Department and other federal departments and agencies joined with Wichita businessmen to hold a two-day meeting in the city in the summer of 1963 to explore ways to get additional government contracts. Many businessmen who have long been dependent on government orders seem to turn almost by instinct to the government for further help when they find themselves in trouble.

The surveys, meetings, and discussions in Wichita resulted not only in new government contracts but also in new industrial plants. Boeing got contracts to carry out necessary modifications on B-52's and to do some work on the Saturn missiles. The Lear Jet Company, manufacturer of small aircraft for business executives and electronic equipment for general use, established a plant in Wichita and within a year was employing four hundred persons. The Coleman Company built a plant for the manufacture of hot water heaters. The existing Cessna plant for the manufacture of small aircraft and the Abbott Laboratories plant expanded their operations. As a result of all these activities, the unemployment rate in Wichita was less than the national average a year after B-52 production ended there.

As in the Presque Isle case, the success in Wichita in meeting the problems caused by a cutback in defense work was due more to the efforts of local businessmen than to any assistance from the federal government. Federal officials acted as advisers and coordinators while the Wichita businessmen did most of their own planning to meet the emergency caused by the end of B-52 production.

For the most part, the successes of the Office of Economic Adjustment have been on a small scale. Nevertheless, the results illustrate many of the problems involved in trying to cut back the size and scope of the military establishment and of defense contracts.

In Decatur, Illinois, a city of seventy-eight thousand in the central part of the state, the Army decided in 1961 to close a Signal Corps depot that consisted of two partly air-conditioned warehouses with more than a million square feet of storage space, large workshops, and office facilities. The depot, located on a 320-acre site, had been built at a cost of $20 million during World War II as a diesel engine factory. Employment at the depot totaled 1,310 when in January 1961 plans were announced by the Army to shut down the installation by April 1962. But the community had been anticipating the closing of the depot and expected a large manufacturing company to locate in the buildings as soon as the government got out of them. Unemployment was high in the area, and the community was anxious to get the Army out of the depot earlier than had been planned. This was arranged, but then the manufacturer decided not to locate in Decatur. Later, however, two other large companies took over the facilities formerly used by the depot and provided enough work to offset the losses caused by the Army's decision to shut down its operations. By 1964, three years after the announcement by the Army of its plans to close the depot, General Electric and Firestone were operating plants in the old depot buildings employing 2,300 persons—almost twice as many as had been working there for the Army.

In York, Pennsylvania, the center of a community of 115,000 in southeastern Pennsylvania, the Navy decided in 1963 to close an ordnance plant that had been employing 1,100 persons. The Navy's timetable called for completing the shutdown by the middle of 1965. To try to ease the impact of its decision, the Navy invited bids from private industry to take over the plant, finish the work scheduled for it by the Navy, and then operate it on its own. The American Machine & Foundry Company got the plant under these conditions with a bid of $9.6 million and increased employment there by 60 percent through the addition of design and engineering work and other diversification. This unusual transaction at York was suggested by the city's businessmen, the first time the Navy had ever sold a plant with the provision that the purchaser would be allowed to complete the work that had been allocated to the facility. In the case of the York plant, this proved to be an excellent way to soften the blow of the transition from a wholly military operation to what it is hoped will eventually be a self-sufficient plant producing only civilian products.

In Greenville, South Carolina, leaders of the community followed much the same course taken by the businessmen at Presque Isle, Maine. When the Air Force announced in 1962 that it was closing the Donaldson Air Base at Greenville, the businessmen and other leaders of the city decided to try to turn the buildings being vacated by the Air Force into industrial plants. As a result of the businessmen's efforts, a chemical plant, a textile mill, a tool and die business, a printer of business forms, and a glider manufacturer set up shop in renovated Air Force buildings. Nearly five thousand new jobs were created both on and off the old Air Force base at Greenville.

In Downey, California, an industrial plant owned by the Air Force was turned into a research, development, and manufacturing center by the National Aeronautics and Space Administration for work on the Apollo, Saturn, and Paraglider projects. In Port Isabel, Texas, a surplus naval air station was taken over by the Justice Department for use as a training school and regional headquarters for agents of the Immigration and Naturalization Service. In Sandusky, Ohio, NASA stepped in again and took over an Army Ammunition Depot to house a reactor, high-energy rocket engine research, and nuclear-rocket dynamics and control work. Greenville, Mississippi, turned an Air Force pilot training center into a municipal airport while Oakland, California, did the same thing with a naval air station. The University of California at San Diego is now using what was once a Marine marksmanship training base while a naval air station at New Iberia, Louisiana, has become a new branch of the Southwestern Louisiana University.

In most of these cases, the federal government's decision to close a defense installation happily coincided with the plans of a community or an industrial firm to locate service, educational, or manufacturing facilities in the vacated buildings or on the abandoned military sites. A few of the communities were fortunate enough to have some warning of the military's plans so that they could make plans of their own to help ease themselves through what otherwise could have been a difficult transition period.

One community that tried to look ahead was Roswell, New Mexico, a city of forty-five thousand that had been highly dependent on an Air Force base and a defense plant. With the emphasis of much of the nation's defense efforts shifting from manned bombers to missiles, the leaders of the Roswell community realized that their city could quickly be in economic difficulties. At the time the city began to examine the base of its prosperity, production at a defense plant that accounted for twenty-five percent of the jobs in the community was being curtailed.

Community meetings as well as discussions with Defense Department officials and officials of other federal agencies led Roswell businessmen to develop plans for expansion of the city's meat-packing and grain-handling facilities as well as the oil and gas production in the area. Further development of Roswell as a wholesale distribution center also seemed advisable as did manufacturing of light aircraft, particularly for foreign markets, efforts to create an electronics industry in the city, and the building of boats and other equipment to take advantage of the boom in outdoor recreation.

In New York, Long Island is a section that has been trying to make plans to offset the cutback in the production of F-105 airplanes at the Farmingdale plant of Republic Aviation Corporation. When the plans for the end of F-105 production were announced in 1962, officials of the Defense Department and other federal agencies helped Long Island businessmen set up the Nassau-Suffolk Economic Development Council to locate new industries and jobs to keep the Long Island economy prosperous. Efforts have been made to expand the already large electronics industry on Long Island as well as to try to get more space contracts for Long Island companies. There has also been considerable talk about the possible development of industries to make use of food and other resources in the sea. In addition, consideration has been given to locating a water desalinization plant on Long Island.

The New York Navy Yard in Brooklyn is another illustration of the need for more advance planning to develop new uses for defense facilities declared surplus by the military. For at least four years before Secretary McNamara's announcement in November 1964 that the Brooklyn yard would be closed, there were strong indications that the yard's days as a Navy facility were limited. Less and less work was going to the yard and employment fell off year after year. But no plans were made either by the Defense Department or by the city government of New York to determine alternate uses for the yard's vast shipbuilding and repairing facilities.

It was not until after the decision to close the yard was announced that efforts were made to draw up plans for its development into a modern industrial enterprise, to be operated either by the city of New York or by private industry. A month after McNamara's decision to shut the yard was made public, a private industrial consulting firm recommended to the New York City Department of Commerce and Industrial Development that the yard be redeveloped by the city as a modern industrial complex or industrial park. A few days later Columbia University professor Melman suggested that the yard could be converted into a commercial shipyard as modern as any facility in the world.

The lack of planning by cities and communities against the day when the military spending that they have depended upon suddenly comes to an end is reflected in the Defense Department itself, where efforts to determine with some precision the economic impact of defense programs began only in 1963. At that time the Institute for Defense Analysis received a Defense Department contract to follow defense spending through its subcontracting stages to find out exactly where all of the department's billions are spent in the economy and what the impact of the expenditures is throughout the nation. Other studies undertaken by the Defense Department included an effort to develop what has been called an "Early Warning System." With such a system the Defense Department would try to project its spending plans over a five-year period and thus be able to warn communities well in advance of changes in spending and weapons development and procurement patterns.

In discussing the work of the Office of Economic Adjustment in testimony before the Senate Subcommittee on Employment and Manpower in 1963, Director Bradford acknowledged the difficulties that the lack of long-range Defense Department planning for changes in military spending had imposed on the already restricted operations of his three-man office.

To try to overcome some of these obstacles, Bradford said, his office had attempted to identify by itself as far in advance as possible some of the more important areas that are likely to be affected by contract changes, had sought to ease the transition, through a process of coordination with leaders in communities affected by contract changes, and then had tried to evaluate carefully each effort to learn from the experience and feed back the results into future programs.

"Even if we believed that defense spending would remain a constant share of U. S. gross national product, or even increase," former Deputy Secretary of Defense Gilpatric told the same subcommittee, "there would still be continual changes in the pattern of procurement within that budget; there would still be shifts in installations and base closings; there would still be program cancellations and completions. Consequently, there would still be the need for localities and industries to readjust to these changes. And even if the defense budget was on the rise, these adjustments would still be painful unless there was a strong and growing national economy which provided opportunities or alternative employment of these resources."

However much the Defense Department officials have recognized the existence of the difficult human and economic problems involved in adjustments to changes in military spending programs, these same officials have neglected the development of plans to deal with the consequences of these changes.

"A program to assist communities, workers, and industries

in adapting to changes in defense spending is essential," said the Senate Subcommittee on Employment and Manpower headed by Senator Clark in a report issued in the spring of 1964. "It must include provisions for early warning from the Department of Defense to communities and industries of impending changes in local defense programs. A series of assistance policies must be devised to help in meeting the temporary problems of local accommodation to these changes. And the federal government must assist defense industry in finding ways to convert its technological capacity and expertise to the civilian sector wherever possible.

"As a result of its hearings in November and December 1963," the report continued, "the subcommittee is by no means convinced that the effective transfer of defense industry technology and management techniques to civilian markets will be simple. These industries have been operating in the past without the cost or sales considerations which prevail in civilian markets. In addition, the rapid innovation to which they have been accustomed is possible only under the very special conditions imposed by national security programs or space exploration. A rate of innovation that rapid in civilian markets might cause serious dislocations in existing industries and employment and would pose special problems for capital financing.

"The subcommittee is optimistic, however," the report said, "that such hurdles can be jumped and has concluded that government and industry together can determine the best techniques for effecting the adaptation of defense technology to civilian needs. The subcommittee has concluded that in addition to such cooperative government-industry approaches, industry should also be afforded some incentive which encourages it to plan for a loss of defense business on its own."

In 1963 the Stanford Research Institute prepared for the Defense Department a report on the problems involved in adjusting industries to shifts in defense spending. The report noted that "defense expenditures are particularly important in precisely those industries, notably electronics and aerospace, that have shown the most rapid pattern of growth and technological innovation in recent years, and have performed the major share of private industry research and development."

The Stanford report concluded that "only a handful of industries and regions would be heavily involved" in major cutbacks in defense spending and said that these would include the large aircraft and missile companies; the suppliers of electronics, propulsion, and other gear for subsystems; instrument manufacturers; and the shipbuilding industry.

"The resources in the affected companies in these regions are highly specialized and would present major problems of reorientation and transfer," the Stanford study pointed out. "The major industrial organizations involved were set up for, and their experience is limited to, the design and production of weapon systems and related aerospace vehicles. Their facilities, especially the manufacturing plant and equipment, have been built for the military market, and alternative economic utilization may be limited. The manpower, in particular, is extremely specialized. Compared with the most technically oriented industry serving commercial markets, the typical defense company may have four or five times the number of scientists and engineers to support a given volume of end-item sales."

The report went on to note that the major defense contractors have been able to move easily from the production of one large, technically-oriented product to another—from aircraft to missiles, as an example—or from one large government market to another—from the military to the space program, for another example. But the Stanford researchers found that the efforts by the contractors to diversify their operations out of nongovernmental areas have not been notably successful.

"Even in the case of companies that have both defense-oriented and commercially-oriented divisions, there appears to be little transference of personnel and product ideas from military to commercial endeavors within the same organization," the Stanford report said. ". . . a given firm's commercial divisions may be hiring engineers at the same time that a military division may be laying off technical personnel. Differences in pay scale and type of experience were cited as barriers to movement from military to commercial work (but not from commercial to military)."

Another problem found by the Stanford researchers was the inability of most defense contractors to believe that there ever will be a serious reduction in military business. The study also discovered a feeling of despair among defense contractors who had tried to produce goods for civilian markets but had failed. "Their previous failures," commented the researchers, "have convinced them that they, and especially their stockholders, would be better off if they just contracted, with the decline in military demand, rather than 'frivolously' dissipating their assets in risky ventures in unrelated fields." The result, said the Stanford report, is that little serious planning for conversion of facilities to peacetime uses is going on in the major defense industries.

The Stanford report went on to note that defense contracts under which manufacturers are guaranteed their costs plus a fixed profit—the cost-plus-fixed-fee contract—have resulted in the companies emphasizing increased quality rather than following the usual business standards of balancing price considerations and quality matters.

"Major defense contractors," the researchers continued, "lack basic marketing capability. This point has been made universally in this and earlier analyses of diversification attempts. The inability of these companies to sell in commercial markets may be too simply termed a lack of marketing capability. It may also indicate the fundamental lack of knowledge of commercial ways of doing business. . . ."

To help defense-oriented companies move into the production of goods for civilian markets, the Stanford report suggested that the federal government could award contracts to them for nondefense research and development work, that some aspects of planning and developing nondefense commercial products could be considered by the government as legitimate defense-contract costs, and that the profit margins on defense contracts, which in general are not large, could be increased to provide the defense contractors with more money for investment in efforts to diversify their operations.

But then, of course, there is always the space program. In its few years of existence it has taken on all of the pork-barrel characteristics of what Senator Fulbright has called "its daddy," the defense program. Congress slowed down the growth of the space program somewhat in 1963 and 1964, but no one in Washington is ready to believe that space spending is going to decline substantially in the near future. It is, as Fulbright has noted, too much of "a grab bag of goodies for everybody." Whenever James E. Webb, the director of the Space Agency, discusses the effects of possible reductions in his budget, he speaks of them in terms of contracts for congressional districts, and members of Congress have no trouble understanding him.

If defense spending declines and the power of the military decreases, space spending could take up the slack in the economy. Some defense contractors are already doing as much business with the Space Agency as with the Pentagon, and others are eyeing space spending as the easiest and most profitable alternative to arms contracts.

But, when viewed in the national interest and in the context of the nation's unmet needs, is the space program indeed the best alternative to heavy defense expenditures? Or are the same seeds of make-work projects that have become a part of the defense program already growing rapidly in the Space Agency?

The economics and politics of the space program deserve careful examination in any discussion of the economic and political repercussions of reductions in defense spending. For some day the space program may be the same unmanageable giant that the defense program became in the late 1950's.

CHAPTER 9

NASA—the New Monster

"IN reflecting on the crash program to reach the moon and the irrational priorities of public policy which it involves," Senator Fulbright told the Senate in November 1963, "I am reminded of the passage in Jonathan Swift's *Gulliver's Travels* in which the author visits the Academy of Projectors in Lagado. The Academy is an institution in which scientists engage in studies and experiments of brilliant inventiveness, which, however, are grotesquely irrelevant to the needs of the destitute society in which they live. One scientist is engaged in a project for extracting sunbeams out of cucumbers, to be put in hermetically-sealed vials and let out to warm the air in raw and rainy summers. Another has devised a method for building houses from the roof downward to the foundations, and another has invented a contrivance by which the most ignorant person would be able to write books on philosophy, poetry, politics, law, mathematics, and theology without having to study.

"The Academy of Lagado, and others like it . . . had become great centers of scientific progress and invention," Fulbright continued. "The only drawback of the great preoccupation with science, Swift points out, is that in the meantime, the whole country lies in waste, the houses are in ruins, and the people are without food and clothes. But far from being discouraged, the people are enormously enthusiastic about the academies and their work and the few troglodytes who persist in living in neat houses and raising edible crops are looked on with contempt as enemies of art, who prefer their own ease and comfort to the general improvement of the country."

Fulbright recalled Gulliver's Academy of Lagado during a Senate debate on appropriations for the National Aeronautics and Space Administration. The Senator noted that since the space program began in 1958 the NASA budget had increased from little more than $100 million a year to over $5 billion and that in a single fiscal year—from 1963 to 1964—the budget went up $1.5 billion, or by almost 50 percent. "I doubt," said Fulbright, "that any other federal program can match NASA's record growth."

The 1963 Senate debate on funds for the Space Agency marked the first time that spending for America's space program had been seriously questioned in Congress even though the NASA budget doubled for two successive years after President Kennedy decided in the spring of 1961 that the United States should try to land a man on the moon by the end of the 1960's.

Never before had the United States government embarked on such an ambitious, costly, and lengthy scientific program. The World War II Manhattan project, which produced the atomic bomb, cost a total of $2.2 billion, less than half what NASA spent for its research and development projects in 1964 alone. The NASA moon project, which accounts for the bulk of the agency's expenditures, is a crash program, but so was the Manhattan project, which was carried out under all of the pressures of wartime. And by the time the United States does land a man on the moon, NASA's Apollo project, as the agency calls its moon program, will have cost at least $20 billion and perhaps as much as $40 billion.

NASA expenditures on research and development, which take up nearly all of the agency's budget, are running close to $5 billion a year, or just $2 billion less than the Defense Department's annual research and development costs of a little more than $7 billion. Most of the military's research and development money has gone into missiles.

The purpose of all the military spending is the defense of the United States and its free world allies, a goal that is not open to question however misdirected some of the military's efforts may have turned out to be. In the case of the space program, however, its goals are confusing and open to serious question.

The scientists involved in the program and many of NASA's supporters on Capitol Hill maintain that the spending for space is simply to advance the frontiers of science. Other persons look on the program as a great adventure, the thrills of which will be vicariously shared by all mankind. Like a mountain, the moon must be explored because it is there. Still others say that the scientific and technological "fallout" from the moon race will benefit man in many ways. Finally, there is the argument that the nation that first plants its flag on the moon will have acquired incalculable prestige. This explanation seems to be the principal reason for the crash United States efforts to put a man on the moon as quickly as possible. For if an American is not the first man to reach the moon, a Russian surely will be.

The economic and political similarities between the defense and space programs are many. Space spending, like military spending, means contracts for businessmen large and small, and contracts mean profits for the businessmen involved and jobs for hundreds of thousands of Americans. James E. Webb, the politically astute administrator of NASA, has estimated that the moon program alone will provide three hundred thousand jobs through the 1960's. Work for NASA is being conducted in universities and industrial plants throughout the country. Although

50 percent of NASA's contracts have been going to California companies, all forty-nine of the other states get some of the Space Agency's money. Ninety percent of the more than $5 billion being spent each year by NASA finds its way to businesses and universities through government contracts, almost all of which are granted following negotiations rather than through competitive bidding.

The largest NASA contractors are also among the biggest defense contractors: North American Aviation, McDonnel Aircraft, Aerojet General, Boeing, Chrysler, Douglas Aircraft, General Dynamics, United Aircraft, Grumman Aircraft, General Electric, Lockheed Aircraft. The transition from the production of military aircraft and missiles to spacecraft and missiles for exploring space is a natural one, so it is not surprising that there should be so much overlapping among the contractors for the two programs.

Most of the contractors that find working for NASA as attractive as they have found defense contracts have done little business except for the government. These companies are the ones that seem to feel at ease only with government contracts and probably would have the greatest difficulty adjusting to production for civilian markets. For many of these companies the space program came along just in time to help take up some of the slack that was beginning to develop in defense as contracts for missiles and other modern weapons were fulfilled and weapons stockpiles reached levels far beyond the nation's defensive or offensive needs.

Taken together, defense and space programs have accounted for 80 percent of all money spent by the federal government for research and development work in recent years. And, it will be recalled, two thirds of all expenditures for research and development in the United States are financed by the federal government.

"It is argued," Fulbright pointed out, "that the space program, like the defense program, is such a great boon to the economy that much harm would come to many important industries and any number of communities if the pace were retarded.

"I am fully aware," the Senator added, "of the significance of the great industries whose financial health is dependent on the space program. With nearly $589 million authorized this year for construction of new facilities related in one way or another to the manned lunar landing program, NASA-supported activities have become major economic factors in many states. Our economy obviously needs stimulation to achieve a higher growth rate, to reduce unemployment, and to bring about utilization of idle productive capacity. The aerospace industries, however, where these billions for the space program will be spent, are not in need of stimulation. A look at the help-wanted section of the classified ads is convincing proof that there is no unemployment problem in space-oriented industries. It is difficult for me to imagine how spending $280 million more in construction of new facilities at Cape Canaveral will ease the lot of an unemployed coal miner or a farmer eking out a bare existence in the Ozarks.

"Expansion of the space program will undoubtedly accentuate existing distortions in the economy brought about by disproportionate concentration of human and physical resources in the defense- and space-oriented industries," Fulbright concluded. "One commentator has said that the significant aspect of the problem is not that 10 percent of the gross national product is devoted to military and space purposes but that three fourths of the engineering and scientific talent of the country is occupied by work in these fields, thus draining away the technological competence that would normally be devoted to civilian purposes. It is interesting to note that only about ... $3.5 million of the present NASA budget is slated for investment in finding ways to adapt knowledge gained through the space program to industrial applications. ... NASA and its contractors have in fact been drawing off large numbers of the most

179

creative scientists and engineers, leaving the less gifted for the civilian-based economy."

During the debate on the NASA appropriations bill in November 1963, Fulbright introduced an amendment to reduce the agency's budget by 10 percent, or a little more than $500 million. He argued that if the moon program and other NASA projects were carried out in a slower, more deliberate manner, costly mistakes such as those that resulted from the crash defense efforts of the 1950's could be avoided. Fulbright also maintained that it would not matter if the United States missed by a few years its goal of putting an American on the moon by the end of the 1960's.

The House and Senate Space Committees as well as the Appropriations Committees of both houses of Congress had already cut back NASA's spending authority by $500 million, but Fulbright and other senators felt that the program was still too large and in danger of getting completely out of hand. For these and other reasons, Fulbright sought further reductions.

Fulbright went on to urge the Senate to use the money that could be saved by his amendment to help meet such needs as education, urban and rural renewal projects, and urban transportation.

"At the risk of being considered something of a troglodyte," Fulbright told the Senate, "I cannot bring myself to believe that going to the moon is essential simply because it is new and creative and adventurous. Still less can I bring myself to believe that the education and welfare of our people warrant lower priorities than space simply because these are old and unimaginative objectives of public policy. The real question before the Congress is not whether we should or should not explore outer space but whether we want to spend seventeen times as much on space adventure this year as on clearing urban blight and slums, whether we want to spend twenty-six times as much on space as on providing adequate public housing for low-income families. These are the essential questions that confront the Senate."

Democratic Senator Clinton P. Anderson of New Mexico, the chairman of the Senate Aeronautical and Space Sciences Committee, and other members of the committee such as Democrats Warren G. Magnuson of Washington, Stuart Symington of Missouri, and John Stennis of Mississippi argued that the space program—and its moon shot—was essential and that the timetable for the crash program would save money rather than waste it.

This argument had also been made by NASA officials in testimony before both the Senate and House Space Committees earlier in the year. The NASA officials maintained that if the program were stretched out it would become more costly because so much of the expense results from the employment of scientists and other supporting staff members needed to make the preparations for a moon shot and back up the men sent to the moon. NASA argues that the longer it takes to prepare for a moon shot the more the Space Agency will have to spend to keep the men concerned with the program on the government payroll.

The trouble with this argument is that the NASA officials seemed to be saying that the agency would be able to reduce its staff and expenditures substantially once the moon shot was successfully completed. But Webb and other NASA officials argued before the congressional Space Committees that most of the agency's activities connected with the moon program would still be carried on even if the moon were abandoned as an immediate target for space exploration.

Among the staunchest defenders of the space program in the Senate are some of the strongest supporters of the military. There is considerable overlapping among the memberships of the Senate Armed Services and Space Committees. Senators Symington and John Sherman Cooper of Kentucky are members of both committees, as are such other friends of the military as Senator Russell, the chairman of the Senate Armed Services Committee, Senator Cannon, and Senator Smith.

After two days of intermittent debate on the Senate floor, Fulbright's amendment to reduce space spending by 10 percent was defeated, but it got a surprising 36 votes, to 46 against it. The 46 to 36 vote was considerably closer than the margins of 4 to 1 and 5 to 1 by which efforts to cut back the military budget were defeated in the Senate both in 1963 and 1964.

There was, as Fulbright had noted, "something . . . for everybody" in the bill, and this made it even more surprising that over a third of the members of the Senate voted for the proposed 10 percent reduction. Just before the vote on his amendment, Fulbright said that "there is so much money in the bill that it would be very embarrassing for any substantial number of representatives and senators to vote to cut it." Pointing to NASA's distribution of research grants, Fulbright said: "Here again there is something for everyone. . . . Everyone gets a little something from NASA. NASA has learned from past experience that it pays to do this. Every state in the union gets substantial research grants, even Arkansas, which has a small part of it in two grants, one for $30,000 and another for $20,000."

Fulbright had also noted that NASA was spending $14 million a year to help finance the education of students at nearly one hundred colleges and universities in almost every state. The Senator said NASA's goal was to aid from three to four thousand students under the program and then finance the postgraduate education of enough of them to graduate one thousand men and women each year with doctoral degrees in the scientific and engineering fields drawn upon by the space program. This would be about a fourth of all the doctoral degrees awarded in these fields annually.

Considering the economic, political, and even scholastic odds working against him, Fulbright, a Rhodes scholar himself as well as a former president of the University of Arkansas, did quite well in getting thirty-five of his colleagues to register a protest against a space program where even the sky is no longer the limit.

When the legislation authorizing NASA's appropriations for the 1965 fiscal year—the figure was $5.2 billion, the same as in the previous year—came before the House in March 1964, Democratic Representative George P. Miller of California, the chairman of the House Space Committee, rested his case on the familiar Capitol Hill catchwords "prestige" and "keeping ahead of the Russians."

"I cannot point to a single national effort," Miller told the House, "that is doing more to offset and counter the many assaults upon our free-world leadership occurring in every corner of the globe than is the space program."

A ranking Republican member of the Space Committee, Representative James G. Fulton of Pennsylvania, agreed with Miller and told the House: "We must realize that Russia, in the current fiscal year, is spending more on space than the United States of America, the richest nation in the world. The Russian people have long since realized the gains economically and in every way—prestige in learning, in stimulation to the universities, colleges, and students, to be attained by space research. At some point, the United States of America must make up its mind: Are we going to sit as an Indian in a teepee in complete ignorance and have this solar system operate as a gigantic machine without our knowing what goes on? ...

"You are being bombarded with tremendous, powerful particles of energy," Fulton warned his colleagues. "Nobody knows where they come from or where they go. They go through you, as you sit here. They go right through without interference. What effect does that have on you? It has affected some of you. If you were to talk to your grandfather, he would say you ought to be locked up, you are out of your mind, or things like that."

Fulton, of course, was talking about cosmic rays and what NASA's scientific research programs could do to solve the mysteries of those rays from outer space. But the members of the House were more interested in such down-to-earth matters as space centers and space contracts. Fulton's colleagues hardly needed to be reminded by him that "the space and rocket industries have grown to be major factors in our economy" and that "the missile and space industry, in dollar volume and people employed, now equals . . . the automobile industry."

"Businessmen, engineers, and communities with chronic and high rates of unemployment and partial use of industries and power," Fulton advised, "should get interested and contact the National Aeronautics and Space Administration procurement agencies. This opportunity in space is open for business, large and small."

In warning against suggestions that the pace of the space program could be slowed down, Democratic Representative Emilio Q. Daddario of Connecticut, another member of the House Space Committee, said that cutbacks in funds would have a serious impact that could not be ignored. "In some areas," said Daddario, "our industrial effort would be merely slowed but in others sharp reductions would need to be made. The peripheral scientific and engineering gains useful to the entire industrial community would likely be lost or reduced."

With these preliminaries out of the way, the House got down to the issue that seemed to be of the greatest interest to most of its members. This was the location of a $50 million electronics research center for the Space Agency. A final decision on the location of the center had been held up for four years because so many members of Congress wanted it.

In 1963 NASA finally decided to place the installation in the Boston area, which with its many colleges and universities and its growing electronics industries seemed to be a logical location for it. But the NASA decision brought protests from members of Congress representing other states that wanted the center. The decision was widely criticized on the grounds that it constituted a political payoff to Democratic Senator Edward M. (Ted) Kennedy.

The protests following NASA's 1963 decision forced the Space Agency to reconsider, and the decision was withdrawn pending further study of the scientific, and political, problems involved in determining the ideal location for the center.

By the spring of 1964 NASA had completed its reevaluation of the situation and, to no one's surprise, announced that its original decision had been the right one. In the view of NASA's administrators Boston was still the ideal location for a $50 million electronics research center.

The decision to locate the electronics research center in the Boston area left a lot of unhappy members of Congress in its wake. Some, however, remained magnanimous about it all.

Republican Representative R. Walter Riehlman of New York was one of those who tried to look at the big space picture. "Although I would very much like it in my own congressional district—and I say that most seriously," Riehlman confessed to his colleagues, "I probably will not have that opportunity to have it. In the final analysis, I am not going to vote against the construction or the initiation of this type of program simply because my district has lost out. This project is more important to the nation than my own feelings. . . .

"This money is not being spent in space, may I say," Riehlman added. "Ninety percent of the money that is being spent in this program is being spent with the industries of the United States of America."

Democratic Representative Roland V. Libonati of Illinois was not quite so magnanimous. He said that the new center was in reality ten centers to study ten major aspects of electronics. Libonati argued that the work of the center should have been divided among ten parts of the country. The Congressman also maintained that his own city of Chicago should have been given a piece of the electronics research center pie because "the Midwest is being denied a participation in federal programs to a point where it hurts."

Another Democratic representative, Ken Hechler of West Virginia, sympathized with complaints such as the one made by Libonati. Hechler was disappointed, too, because the electronics research center had not gone to his state, which he said "has been shortchanged when it comes to NASA prime contracts, and even subcontracts. We are way down near the bottom of the heap. . . . We are lower down than the Midwest."

Democratic Representative John Brademas of Indiana was unhappy because "the concentration of defense and space spending on the eastern, western, and southern coasts of the United States is leading to a serious unbalancing of the economy of the nation as a whole.

"Studies sponsored by the Defense Department itself," Brademas continued, "have made clear that federal research and development carried out in those areas have led to production contracts, generating in turn greater economic activity in those regions of the country.

"I hope," the Congressman concluded, "that NASA will pay far more attention to the talents and abilities of the Midwest in the future than it has in the past. We pay taxes, too."

Republican Representative Fred Schwengel of Iowa declared that "the heart and soul" of his congressional district went into the preparation of a prospectus arguing for the location of the electronics research center in Iowa. Schwengel maintained that NASA's reevaluation of the location of the center was mere "window-dressing" because "commitments are commitments, and campaign promises are not made to be broken."

Only the members of the Massachusetts delegation had kind words for NASA's decision. Democratic Representative Harold D. Donohue arose to say: "Most sincerely I commend the scientific judgment of those recognized authorities who recommended and approved this location. I have long advocated, individually and cooperatively, placement of this research facility in Massachusetts, whose abundantly skilled workers and established electronic resources preeminently assure its successful operation. In accord with the most patriotic motivations, in compliance with the most economic standards, and in response to the most authoritative scientific recommendations this research center ought to be, in the national interest, located within the great Commonwealth of Massachusetts and I trust its construction will be speedily initiated."

So the debate on the space program went that afternoon in March 1964. At one point Democratic Representative Joseph E. Karth of Minnesota summed it all up well when he observed that "it does appear there is not too much interest in the general debate on this bill." The only issue that generated any interest was the electronics research center, and the issue was considered only in terms of which state should get this economic and political plum. It was like the perennial debates on Defense Department appropriations in which more time was spent in arguing over how the Navy's funds were to be divided between its own shipyards and those operated by private companies than over any substantive questions of basic defense policies. And, like the defense appropriations bills, the legislation providing money for NASA's operations was approved intact by the House.

Three months later, in June 1964, Senator Fulbright made another effort in the Senate to reduce the cost of the space program and get Congress to reappraise the goal of trying to land a man on the moon by the end of the 1960's. Fulbright sponsored an amendment to the bill authorizing NASA's appropriations which would have cut back the Apollo moon program by $267 million.

"Stated in its simplest terms," said Fulbright, "the question is whether or not Congress believes it more important for this nation to put a man on the moon and return him to earth within the decade or that we take care of some of the pressing problems on earth whose solution may make our society stronger and life for our people more meaningful."

Fulbright's arguments for his amendment were much the same as those he had made the previous November in seeking Senate approval of a considerably more ambitious amendment that would have cut back the space budget by 10 percent. The Senate liked his proposal only slightly more in June than it had in November. In June, thirty-eight senators voted for the cutback in space funds proposed by Fullbright, but forty-three senators voted against it. The thirty-eight votes for Fulbright's second proposal was, however, a gain of two votes over his previous effort.

Most members of Congress seem to take the same pork-barrel view of the space program as they do of defense spending. The space program is by no means as large as defense spending, but its economic and political benefits are the same. Nearly all of the space budget is immediately translated into contracts that are as eagerly sought by businessmen and by communities as are defense contracts. And once the work called for by a space or defense contract is under way, the economic and political pressures begin to build up to keep the program going at all costs and to expand it if at all possible.

In the case of NASA, as in the case of the Defense Department, members of Congress tend to give the spending programs only a cursory annual review. Volumes of testimony are taken, but practically all of it comes from NASA officials or contractors who have a vested interest in keeping the agency's programs as large and as lengthy as possible.

"It seems to me that 90 percent of what we are doing is sitting piously and solemnly listening to a lot of stuff that means nothing to us, and we are not getting really vital information,"

Republican Senator Clifford P. Case of New Jersey said during the 1964 Senate hearings on the space program.

During the same hearings Senator Keating noted that NASA Administrator Webb had emphasized the possible technological fallout from the space program in his 1964 testimony while a year earlier he had stressed the manned space flight aspects of the program. In both years, of course, the directions and goals of the program were supposed to be the same, with the only difference being that NASA's basic projects presumably were more advanced in 1964 than they were in 1963. But, as Webb well knew, within the period of a year the moon program had been widely criticized and seriously questioned even by many scientists who previously were thought to have been sympathetic with most of NASA's operations.

"Your stress this year," Keating said to Webb, "is not so much on the manned space flight, but on the subsidiary gains from the space programs in technology and so on. Last year the technology was the last part of your presentation. I gained the impression it was tacked on to the talk about manned space flight. This year technology utilization was discussed first and at length. I like that. I think also it is shrewd on your part to change your emphasis."

In replying to Keating, Webb acknowledged that "part of the product of these presentations is the questions asked by the committee, and we, to some extent, emphasize the things that come up."

In only six years the Senate and House Space Committees have become as much a part of what could be called the space-industrial complex as the Armed Services Committees are of the military-industrial complex. The rewards are the same in both cases—contracts and jobs and of course profits, too, for businesses and communities throughout the nation.

As the history of the defense program has shown since World War II, and particularly in the twelve years since the end of the Korean War, Congress seems to have gotten out of the habit of closely scrutinizing and questioning programs that, however essential they may be to national defense or to the nation's prestige, still can breed inefficiency and waste. Congress appears to be incapable of grappling with the many difficult problems that arise from the very nature of large governmental operations like the space program or the defense program.

From time to time, aspects of both the defense and space programs have become so intolerable that congressional committees have conducted careful investigations of matters like the stockpiling program. Often, however, the investigations stem from complaints of disgruntled contractors or members of Congress who feel that they have been discriminated against and have not received what they regard to be their fair share of government contracts.

The political and economic pressures for programs involving large government contracts will continue as long as there do not seem to be any viable political and economic alternatives to them. A new member of Congress soon learns that contracts are a political asset that he often will be privileged to announce to his constituents, and old members of Congress have long since learned the political advantages inherent in the ever-growing number of programs that offer money and jobs to their constituents.

To alleviate these political and economic pressures the federal government must provide attractive political programs as alternatives to defense and space spending that is no longer needed. Otherwise, the pressures will continue and more and more defense and space programs will turn into make-work projects.

CHAPTER 10

To Plan for Peace

"MOST important of all, let us openly and frankly recognize the defense adjustment problem," Senator Clark told a meeting of the Electronics Industries Association in March 1964. "Let us insist upon open discussion and study in Congress. In the past we have done a good job planning for war. Should not we have the sense also to plan for peace and prosperity? If we don't we are apt to end up with neither.

"Suddenly," Clark continued, "as we find the strategic weapons systems we have developed going into place in concrete silos we have awakened to what we should have known all along: that now, as the massive strategic systems are falling into place, the 'forced draft' engendered by defense spending will ease a little and the defense industry will then have to search for fresh breezes blowing from the domestic quarters of the economy. And those breezes are far gentler than those generated in the artificial wind tunnel of defense."

Clark suggested that the Defense Department expedite development of an "Early Warning System" to forecast shifts in military spending; retraining and other economic assistance programs be extended to areas where defense spending falls off;

systematic studies be made of potential uses for abandoned military installations; and states, cities, and industries themselves make long-range plans for adjusting to cutbacks in the defense program.

An office with a full-time director and a substantial staff should be set up on the White House level to evaluate and develop programs to ease the economic and political shock of disarmament. Such an office would function best in an independent position rather than as part of the Defense or Commerce Departments where it might easily be swallowed up in the existing bureaucracy. The office should begin its work by carrying out some of the studies suggested by both Senators Clark and McGovern.

The office must, however, do much more than merely conduct studies, valuable as they may be as a starting point. The office should draw up plans for expanding such programs as unemployment compensation, manpower retraining, aid to depressed areas, small business loans, and public works grants so that they can be used to help areas and industries converting from defense contracts to production for the civilian economy.

New proposals for economic aid should also be considered. Moving allowances should be provided by the government to help persons thrown out of work by the loss of a defense contract or the closing of a military base. Such allowances have been used successfully to give workers easier mobility in Britain and Sweden. A program of government loans and grants should also be set up to help defense contractors buy new machinery and make other changes in their plants to ease conversion problems.

Another problem that urgently needs examination is the likely extent and scope of a disarmament industry. It has been suggested by some advocates of disarmament that an arms control agreement would lead to the development of a rather large and sophisticated industry to build and operate the many devices that would be needed to police a worldwide disarmament agreement. These would include devices to detect the testing of nuclear weapons and determine whether there is an unusual movement of men and matériel.

But no one really knows whether the inspection procedures required to police a disarmament agreement would be of such magnitude as to create a vast new industry. The answer to this question may depend on unresolved debates over future military strategy, but the investigation of the possible size and scope of a disarmament industry ought to be made—and the results made public.

Such a program of research into the effects of cutbacks in defense spending and the development of methods of aiding workers, companies, and communities caught up in reductions in military spending cannot succeed, however, unless the nation's economy is operating at a high and sustained level of prosperity.

Also of crucial importance is leadership from the President recognizing the difficulties inherent in a reconversion program as well as the need to channel most of the money saved by reductions in defense spending to other government programs designed to meet some of the essential civilian needs shortchanged during the long years of heavy military expenditures.

The longer we delay planning and educational efforts to ease the transition to an economy considerably less dependent on military spending the more deeply embedded will be the idea that large defense expenditures are essential to the well-being of the United States economy. The present pause in the arms race ought to be welcomed, not feared, by Americans. It will be a period of change, but it does not need to be a time of peril unless the President fails to take the lead in telling the American people about the opportunities flowing from such a change.

Two important aspects of the expertise developed by the defense and space industries would be of considerable help in working out solutions to many problems in the rest of the economy. One is the experience of these industries in carrying out complex research and development problems. They know how to apply research efforts in such an intensive way that the results can be immediately applied to problems at hand.

The other aspect of defense and space work is "systems engineering" or the "systems approach" to the solving of problems. This kind of engineering looks at a problem as a whole rather than at its isolated parts, and seeks a solution to the entire problem. In the field of civilian air transportation, for example, systems engineering would include the problems of getting from one's home or office to the airport, the handling of baggage, the processing of tickets, and the movement of the passenger from the airport terminal to the plane itself as well as the development of faster and safer airplanes.

In testimony before the Senate Employment and Manpower subcommittee in the fall of 1963, Michael Michaelis of the engineering consulting firm of Arthur B. Little, Inc., noted that the American Telephone & Telegraph Company has developed the world's outstanding communications network by always thinking in terms of a system rather than only about the component parts of a system.

"How different this seems," Michaelis said, "from the way in which we transport not words and pictures but actual people and goods. Here we arrange our affairs in such a way that corporate entities are generally restricted to one specific technical mode of transportation, be it railroads, airlines, trucks, ships, or pipelines. Hence, we find a lack of systems thinking and planning."

Michaelis pointed out that he had discussed with engineers devices on drawing boards that are a mix between rail and air transportation, "a mix in the sense that it involves a 'flying' vehicle that travels along a right-of-way on the ground and requires advanced aeronautical designs to achieve speeds of several hundreds of miles per hour." In his 1965 State of the Union message, President Johnson asked Congress to appropriate funds for a study of a new transportation system from Washington to Boston that would include an examination of such flying vehicles.

Michaelis also suggested that systems engineering could be applied to the construction industry where many new ideas are slow to be adapted because of the fragmented nature of the industry.

The defense industry's experience with research and development and systems engineering are but two examples of the military expertise that could be readily adapted to problems of the civilian economy.

In the United States the problems confronting the domestic economy are those of a generally prosperous society that has become urbanized too fast and with too little planning. They are the problems of city slums, of getting people to and from work at better than horse-and-buggy speeds, of cleaning up the streams and air polluted by modern civilization, of giving all of today's children an education commensurate with the needs of today's world, of preserving natural beauty where it remains in the countryside, and of reintroducing beauty to the cities that have destroyed it. There is much work to be done with the money that would be made available by the reduction of military expenditures.

Nevertheless, drastic changes in the patterns of defense spending and sharp reductions in the cost of defense programs would create fundamental political and economic problems for the United States. The transition from an economy with a large defense program to one with a considerably smaller military effort would naturally be resisted by the generals and the admirals, the businessmen, the union leaders, and all the others who have an understandable interest in a continued high level of defense spending. They would be joined by members of Congress who have a political interest in keeping defense spending as it is and also by the leaders of communities heavily dependent on large military budgets.

But with strong leadership from the President it would be possible to turn changes and reductions in the defense program into great opportunities. The importance of presidential leadership in such an undertaking cannot be stressed too much, however, because of the strength of the forces with an overriding economic interest in maintaining the defense status quo.

That is why advance planning is so crucial. Alternatives to continued high defense spending must be available to resist the inevitable pressures against change in military expenditures. Under even the most favorable circumstances, the transition from a high level of defense spending to a lower plateau would be difficult and harmful to the immediate economic interests of many Americans as well as to many governmental institutions and private corporations.

But it would be even worse to try to turn the defense program into what President Johnson has called "a WPA nuclear project." Yet the dangers of doing that are ever present so long as there are no plans and no adequate government machinery for easing the nation over the periods of transition and conversion.

The economic and political problems of changes and reductions in the defense program—and of course of disarmament, however far off that may be—are in the words of Senator McGovern "a test of the political maturity of the American people."

It is a test in which all of us will be guinea pigs, and it is also a test that will be anxiously watched by the rest of the world. For the United States will be called upon to demonstrate to the entire world whether it can adjust to peace as easily as it can tool up for war.

Sources

THIS book is based on material from Defense Department statements and reports, General Accounting Office reports, the official proceedings of the Senate and the House as recorded in the *Congressional Record*, reports and hearings of the Senate and House Armed Services, Appropriations, Space, and Government Operations Committees, the Senate Labor and Commerce Committees, the Joint Economic Committee, and interviews by the author with Defense Department officials, members of Congress, and private citizens who have worked for the Defense Department or have been involved in various aspects of defense contracting.

CHAPTER 1

The 1964 Senate debate on the bill authorizing military appropriations for the 1965 fiscal year is on pages 3584–86, 3602–04, 3678–88, and 3690–99 of the 1964 *Congressional Record*. (All *Congressional Record* pages references are to the daily edition.) The 1963 Senate debate over military appropriations is on pages 17865–94 of the 1963 *Record*. The 1964 House debate on the defense appropriations bill can be found on pages 8494–538 of the 1964 *Record*, and the debate on the bill in the Senate on pages 16779–830. Representative Brademas' discussion of Studebaker's defense contracts is on pages 22751–52 of the 1963 *Record* and Senator Mansfield's discussion of waste in the defense program is on pages 23352–56 of the 1963 *Record*.

CHAPTER 2

The most complete account of the Big Dish project is in an April 1964 GAO report: "Unnecessary Costs Incurred for the Naval Radio Research Station Project at Sugar Grove, W. Va." For additional material on the project, see the 1963 *Congressional Record*, pages 19091–96. *Science* magazine discussed the project in its May 29, 1964, issue. A discussion of the $300 million missile system that never worked can be found in a February 1964 GAO report: "Unclassified Summary of Findings in Classified Report on Development, Procurement and Deployment of an Unsatisfactory Missile System." The details of the seaplane that never flew are in a March 1964 GAO report: "Additional Costs Incurred in the Procurement of P6M Seaplanes from Glenn L. Martin Co., Baltimore, Md." An exhaustive study of the nuclear airplane project was published by the GAO in February 1963: "Review of Manned Aircraft Nuclear Propulsion Program." Information on the SAGE system may be found on page 453 of the 1963 hearings of the House Defense Appropriations subcommittee.

CHAPTER 3

For an account of President Johnson's California speech, see The Washington *Star*, June 19, 1964: "California Gains Recounted by Johnson as Tour Opens." For Mr. Johnson's NASA speech, see *The New York Times*, April 24, 1963: "What Government Officials Do You Believe?" A good account of NASA's Manned Spacecraft Center at Houston appeared in *The New York Times*, October 6, 1963: "Moon Race Spurs Boom in Houston." Senator Gordon Allott (Republican, Colorado) discussed the A-11 airplane at some length and his remarks are on pages 7788–93 of the 1964 *Congressional Record*. Secretary McNamara's testimony before the Democratic Platform Committee is on pages A4442–44 of the 1964 *Record* and former Secretary Gates' letter critical of McNamara is on page 22458. Vice President Humphrey's pledge to help the American aircraft industry was reported in *The New York Times*, October 2, 1964: "Air Industry Gets a Pledge of Help." Former Representative Miller's criticisms were reported in the issue of October 27: "Miller

Charges Defense Politics." Senator Murphy's remarks can be found in press releases issued on September 17 and 27, 1964, by the George Murphy for United States Senate Committee. Representative Wilson's rebuttal is on pages 22416–17 of the 1964 *Congressional Record.* Senator Bennett's speech is on pages 22559–60 of the 1964 *Record.* The account of the Council for a Livable World is based on the author's: "Obscure Disarmament Group Is Political Issue in West," in The Washington *Post,* October 26, 1964. Robert S. Allen and Paul Scott reported on the 1960 Republican clearing committee in their Washington column on April 21, 1960. For an account of how contracts are announced, see the *Wall Street Journal,* October 14, 1963: "The Guided Leak," and The Washington *Post,* March 11, 1963: "Tipoffs Let Congressmen Accept Contracts Credit." The account of the MMRBM is based on interviews by the author.

CHAPTER 4

For statistics and other information on the size and economic impact of defense spending, see the 1963 and 1964 hearings and reports of the Subcommittee on Defense Procurement of the Joint Economic Committee: "Impact of Military Supply and Service Activities on the Economy." The U.S. Arms Control and Disarmament Agency's report, published in January 1962, is entitled: "Economic Impacts of Disarmament." The testimony by Gilpatric, Wiedenbaum, and Rubel may be found both in *Nation's Manpower Revolution,* Hearings, Part Seven, Subcommittee on Employment and Manpower of the Senate Labor and Public Welfare Committee and in Volume Two of *Selected Readings* compiled for the subcommittee: "Convertibility of Space and Defense Resources to Civilian Needs: A Search for New Employment Potentials." Both the hearings and the volume of readings were published in 1964. The shifts in defense spending are detailed in: "Five-Year Trends in Defense Procurement, 1958–1962," a booklet published in June 1963 by the Office of the Secretary of Defense. Former President Truman's letters on negotiated contracts as well as other material on changes in contracting procedures can be found in: "Economic Aspects of Military Procurement and Supply," Report of the Subcommittee on Defense Procurement to the Joint Economic Committee, October 1960. The

1963 and 1964 hearings of the Defense Procurement subcommittee, cited above, contain many examples of savings in defense costs. The employment of retired commissioned officers by Defense Department contracts is discussed in a 1960 report on H. Res. 19 by the Subcommittee for Special Investigations of the House Armed Services Committee. For an account of the Defense Advisory Council see: "New Council Solves Pentagon-Industry Defense Problems," The Washington *Post*, March 20, 1963. The details of the Western Electric investigation are in: "Pyramiding of Profits and Costs in the Missile Procurement Case," Hearings, Permanent Subcommittee on Investigations of the Senate Government Operations Committee, Parts 1 and 2, published in 1962, and in Senate Report 970, 88th Congress, Second Session, March 31, 1964.

CHAPTER 5

For a discussion of the Secretary of Defense's job and McNamara's achievements, see: "Revolution in the Pentagon," by Theodore H. White, *Look* magazine, April 23, 1963. For an account of the activities of the "fearless four," see pages 3094–3100 of the 1964 *Congressional Record*. The 1963 Air Force Association statement can be found on pages 16060–62 of the 1963 *Record*. For an account of the Association's activities, see: "Rebellion in the Air Force?" by Raymond D. Senter, *The New Republic*, September 28, 1963. An account of the effort to put the Nike-Zeus on the production lines is in the *Congressional Quarterly* weekly report of March 13, 1961, one of the first attempts to document former President Eisenhower's statements about the dangers of the "military-industrial complex." For details on the Navy yards, see *The New York Times* for November 20, 1964. For the complicated TFX story, see: "TFX Contract Investigation," Hearings, Permanent Subcommittee on Investigation of the Senate Government Operations Committee, Parts 1–10, 1963. Secretary McNamara's documentation of savings in the defense program is contained in: "Memorandum for the President: Department of Defense Cost Reduction Program—Second Annual Progress Report," issued by the Office of the Secretary of Defense on July 7, 1964. It is also reprinted in "Economic Impact of Federal Supply and Service Activities," Report of the Subcommittee on Defense Procurement to the Joint Economic Committee, published in September 1964. Admiral Anderson's speech can be found on pages A5617–19 of the 1963 *Congressional Record*.

CHAPTER 6

Details of the stockpile program can be found in: "Inquiry into the Strategic and Critical Material Stockpiles of the United States," Draft Report of the National Stockpile and Naval Petroleum Reserves Subcommittee of the Senate Armed Services Committee, published in 1963. The Joint Committee on Reduction of Nonessential Federal Expenditures, headed by Senator Harry F. Byrd (Democrat, Virginia), issues monthly reports on the size of the stockpile and they are printed regularly in the *Congressional Record*.

CHAPTER 7

The House debate over additional funds for the Arms Control and Disarmament Agency is recorded on pages 21413–46 of the 1963 *Congressional Record*. The Senate debate on awarding defense contracts to depressed areas is on pages 17872–86 of the 1963 *Record*. Humphrey's 1962 speech on the study the Foreign Relations Committee would not make public is on pages 22558–64 of the 1962 *Record*. Professor Melman's pamphlet was reprinted in the May 4, 1963 issue of the *Saturday Review*. The details of Senator McGovern's proposal for a National Economic Conversion Commission can be found on pages 19723–42 of the 1963 *Record* as well as in: "National Economic Conversion Commission," Hearings Before the Senate Commerce Committee, published in 1964. The details of the National Economic Conversion Committee set up by President Johnson in December 1963 are on pages 24423–27 of the 1963 *Record*.

CHAPTER 8

Two Defense Department pamphlets, "Community Economic Adjustment Program," published in 1963 and "Productive Civilian Uses of Former Defense Department Installations," published in 1964, contain considerable material on the background and accomplishments of the Office of Economic Adjustment. There is further information in the Hearings and Readings of the Senate Employment and Manpower subcommittee cited above in the sources for Chapter 4. Also see: "Toward Full Employment: Proposals for a Comprehensive Employment and Manpower Policy in the United States," the subcommittee's report published in April 1964. The Stanford Research Institute report may also be found in the subcommittee's Hearings.

CHAPTER 9

Senator Fulbright's efforts to reduce spending on the space program are recorded on pages 21275–99 and 21347–73 of the 1963 *Congressional Record* and pages 14367–84 of the 1964 *Record*. The 1964 House debate on the program may be found on pages 6077–6123 of the 1964 *Record*. The hearings of both the Senate and the House Space Committees provide excellent insights into the way members of Congress view the space program.

CHAPTER 10

The Michaelis testimony is in the Senate Manpower subcommittee hearings mentioned above in the sources for Chapter 4.

FOR FURTHER READING

Other recent books discussing these and related problems include: *The Economics of Defense in the Nuclear Age,* by Charles J. Hitch and Roland N. McKean (Cambridge, 1960); *The Warfare State,* by Fred J. Cook (New York, 1962); *Disarmament and the Economy,* edited by Emile Benoit and Kenneth E. Boulding (New York, 1963); *The Weapons Acquisition Process,* by Merton J. Peck and Frederick M. Scherer (Boston, 1962); *The Military Establishment,* by John M. Swomley, Jr. (Boston, 1964); *The Passion of the Hawks,* by Tristram Coffin (New York, 1964); *Power at the Pentagon,* by Jack Raymond (New York, 1964); *The Age of Deterrence,* by George E. Lowe (Boston, 1964); and *The McNamara Strategy,* by William W. Kaufmann (New York, 1964).

Index

Farbstein, Leonard, 134
Federal Aviation Agency, 36
Flemming, Arthur S., 119, 124-125, 129
Flood, Daniel J., 35, 95
Ford, Gerald R., Jr., 53, 59
Ford's Aeronautical Division, 57
Foreign Affairs magazine, 137
Forrestal, James V., 87
Freeport Sulphur Company, 129
Fruehauf Corporation, 78-80
Fulbright, J.W., amendment on space appropriation, 187-188; economics of space spending, 178-190; military-industrial complex, 17-18; on Space Agency, 173; Senate appropriations for NASA, 175-176, 180-183
Fulton, James G., 183-184

Gates, Thomas S., Jr., 42, 87
Gemini, 91
General Accounting Office, Aircraft Nuclear Propulsion Program, 29, 31-33; army missile, 25-26; Big Dish, 22-23; P6M seaplane, 26-29
General Dynamics Corporation, 40, 43, 65, 74, 101, 103, 178
General Electric, 65, 178
General Precision, 57
Gilpatric, Roswell L., on defense budget, 65-66, 76, 137-138, 169
Goldwater, Barry M., 7, 41, 57
Goodrich, B.F. Company, 126
Greenville, South Carolina, Air Base, 165-166
Gross National Product, defense program as percentage of, 62-63
Grumman Aircraft, 52, 53, 55-56, 178

Halaby, Najeeb E., 36
Hanna, M.A., Company, 127-128
Harding, Ralph R., 47
Hart, Philip, 49, 136; Commission on the Application of Technology to Community & Manpower Needs, 151
Hartke, Vance, 14-15
Hayden, Carl, 56-57
Hébert, F. Edward, 74-75
Hechler, Ken, 186
Henney Motor Company, 80
Hitch, Charles J., 90

Hosmer, Craig, 133-135
House Appropriations Committee, 87-91
House Armed Services Committee, 8-9, 87-91, 181-182
Hughes Aircraft, 56, 57
Humphrey, George M., 119, 127-128
Humphrey, Hubert H., 42-43; Commission on Automation, Technology and Employment, 150-151; on disarmament, 136-137

Ichord, Richard H., 88
Inventories, defense department, 104-105
Institute for Defense Analysis, 155-156, 168

Jackson, Henry M., 43, 103
Johnson, Louis A., 87
Johnson, Lyndon B., campaign of 1964, 39, 40; on A-11, 41; on Committee on the Economic Impact of Defense and Disarmament, 151-152; on contract announcements, 55, 98; on Council for a Livable World, 48
Jordan, B. Everett, 95
Jupiter missile, 87

Karth, Joseph E., 187
Keating, Kenneth B., 48, 53, 189
Keefe, James K., 162
Kennedy, Edward M., 52-53, 164-165
Kennedy, John F., 1960 campaign, 40-41, 98; on military base closings, 158-159; on stockpiling, 114-115, 145
Kennedy, Robert F., 48
Kerr, Robert S., 102
Kilgore, Joe M., 103
King, David, 48-49
Kirwan, Mike, 11
Kuchel, Thomas H., 135

Lead and zinc, 116-121
LeMay, Curtis S., 8-9
Libonati, Roland V., 185-186
Linton, Ron, 59
Little, Arthur B., Inc., 194